THE MARITAL KNOT

Praises for *The Marital Knot*

This amazing book by an émigré Indian psychiatrist and psychoanalyst, describes the emotional roller coaster of arranged marriages and their cultural context. Charting her and her patient's immigrant experience, she discusses such marriages, the rare difficult divorces, and the western dating scene with its challenges post divorce. She gives us a fascinating view of another culture and also our own. She discusses deeply and profoundly the issue of commitment; its phenomenology, constraints, inhibitions, indulgences, abuses and benefits. This book will interest and help all who are, wish to be or were married. A must read book I recommend highly and warmly!

—**Eric R. Marcus**, MD, Director, Columbia University Center for
Psychoanalytic Training and Research. Professor of Clinical Psychiatry,
Columbia University College of Physicians and Surgeons

Shabnamzehra Bhojani's *The Marital Knot* represents a significant and highly original contribution to the psychoanalytic study of marriage. Dr. Bhojani utilizes a psychoanalytic lens in this lucidly written and thought provoking study of both arranged marriages and traditional love marriages. Theory is combined with case illustrations in this superb analysis of the rupture /repair cycle grappled with by every couple in a long term relationship. The enemies of repair, including envy, rage, hate and evil, are explored and followed by the role played by empathy, forgiveness and mourning in marital security, healing and growth. *The Marital Knot* will serve as a most welcome addition to the literature and of great interest and value to a professional audience as well as all lay readers seeking a deeper understanding of the psychodynamics of the marital relationship … their own, their patients' and all others.

—**Dr. Steven A. Luel**, Ed.D.,L.P, Developmental Psychologist.
Assoc. Professor of Education and Psychology,
Touro College, New York

In *The Marriage Knot*, Dr. Bhojani explores the deeply personal and problematic experiences of arranged and love marriages. We see the crises posed by family, culture, commitment, hate, violence, divorce and love. We travel into her world of arranged marriages, and then to love marriages. She shows us the pain, loss, repair and ultimately, of healing that is possible through psychoanalytic therapy, for both patient and analyst. As she makes very clear, the ties that bind should be neither too tight nor too loose. They should be strong, but not hurtful, and made of loving commitment. Dr. Bhojani reminds us how hard it can to be get the marriage knot to fit just right and how lucky when we can. I found myself viewing my personal history and my professional life with an enriched vision.

—**Robert Alan Glick,** MD, Professor of Clinical Psychiatry, Columbia University. Former Director of the Columbia University Center for Training and Research

THE
MARITAL
KNOT
Arranged Marriages, Love Marriages &
the Ties that Bind

Shabnamzehra Bhojani
—MD, F.A.P.A.—

NEW YORK

NASHVILLE • MELBOURNE • VANCOUVER

THE MARITAL KNOT
Arranged Marriages, Love Marriages & the Ties that Bind

© 2018 **Shabnamzehra Bhojani, MD, F.A.P.A.**

Published in New York, New York, by Morgan James Publishing. Morgan James is a trademark of Morgan James, LLC. www.MorganJamesPublishing.com

The Morgan James Speakers Group can bring authors to your live event. For more information or to book an event visit The Morgan James Speakers Group at www.TheMorganJamesSpeakersGroup.com.

ISBN 978-1-68350-657-7 paperback
ISBN 978-1-68350-658-4 eBook
Library of Congress Control Number: 2017910313

Cover Design by:
Rachel Lopez
www.r2cdesign.com

Interior Design by:
Bonnie Bushman
The Whole Caboodle Graphic Design

In an effort to support local communities, raise awareness and funds, Morgan James Publishing donates a percentage of all book sales for the life of each book to Habitat for Humanity Peninsula and Greater Williamsburg.

Get involved today! Visit
www.MorganJamesBuilds.com

Dedication

For my son Abbas who I love more than words can express, and who permitted his mother to spend so much time writing this book. And for my father Pyarali and especially for my mother Rukkaiya, who has given so much and received so little.

Table of Contents

Introduction

I am an immigrant from India, and I was in an arranged marriage. I am also a practicing psychiatrist, child psychiatrist and psychoanalytic candidate in training, and my practice has been fundamentally shaped by my status as an immigrant and by my divorce—legal and religious— from the husband who was chosen for me. My choice of topics for this book has been informed by these experiences and my understanding of theories related to these experiences and by the following question: How does one form a lasting (and quality) marriage in a society where one is free to choose one's partner, vs. where one is restricted from this freedom and where divorcing that partner is relatively difficult? Divorce in freely chosen marriages is easy compared to divorce in arranged marriages— especially for women.

When I mention to friends and colleagues that I was in an arranged marriage, the typical response is disbelief that anyone would willingly submit to such a thing. The most common question is, how could you possibly know that you love him? This is exacerbated when they discover that in arranged marriages it is common for the spouses-to-be to meet only once or twice before the wedding. Physical contact is out of the question, a fact that Americans find particularly consternating. When I tell them that my own arranged marriage—like Sarah's—occurred after I had arrived in America, this only increases their incredulousness. I often perceive an attitude of disdain or even contempt for the very idea that one does not freely choose his spouse. Sometimes this disdain is subtle in its expression, sometimes not so much.

I had the good fortune to treat a patient ("Sarah") whose experience had many similarities to mine. Sarah emigrated from Pakistan and upon arrival in the U.S. a husband was chosen for her. She met him once, they married, and then quickly divorced once Sarah realized how incompatible they were. It was not long into her treatment when I realized that both of us were dealing with some of the same issues. First, both of us had a difficult time dealing with our extended families, who did not look favorably on us for divorcing our husbands. Second, divorce from an arranged marriage—for a woman—is no easy feat. Third, after divorcing the husbands who were chosen for us by male family members, we were left to negotiate the American "dating scene." For many people, Sarah and I included, the "dating scene" is ultimately a marriage market.

Lastly, after divorcing our husbands we found it necessary to reinvent ourselves. This was a matter of survival in a culture so radically different from the ones in which we had been raised. Second, the longer I was in the U.S. the more I felt it necessary to choose what aspects of my Indian heritage to keep and what aspects of American culture I wanted to incorporate as part of my identity. Sarah went through a similar process with respect to her Pakistani identity. These two existential processes of reinventing ourselves are distinct but intimately related.

This book begins by recounting Sarah's experiences as an immigrant and as a woman who divorced her husband from an arranged marriage. Next I turn to the issue of commitment, which has become important to me personally. In arranged marriages, commitment is not an issue like it is in America or the West generally. The word for commitment is rarely if ever used with respect to marriage; that the couple will stay together until death is assumed. The marriage bond is enforced by the immediate family, the extended family, the community, and the patriarchal nature of societies where arranged marriages are the norm.

Traditional societies like India and Pakistan, especially in rural areas that have not been influenced by Western society, are extremely patriarchal. Friends and colleagues are invariably shocked and outraged by my stories of what is normal behavior in an Indian arranged marriage. Virtually all the power is in the hands of the husband and his male relatives. For example, a man can divorce his wife for the most trivial reasons, but a woman does not have this right. In rural India, it is extremely difficult for a woman to get a divorce. It should come as no surprise that extreme patriarchy is accompanied by pervasive domestic violence; in general, the only way for a woman to get a divorce in rural India is to demonstrate that she has been the victim of serial and extreme domestic violence. Moreover, a woman who succeeds in divorcing her husband has won a pyrrhic victory, because divorced women are stigmatized and have little hope of remarrying. Men automatically get custody of the children, and are not required to pay alimony of any kind.

It should come as no surprise that divorce initiated by the wife is rare in a society like rural India. Many factors work to keep the married couple together, no matter how unpleasant the relationship between husband and wife. Again, "commitment" simply is not a relevant concept. Only in a society where marriage partners are freely chosen, and divorce is relatively easy, does commitment become an important concept. Though the divorce rate in America is high, marriage is as popular as ever, a combination that accounts for the American obsession with commitment and how to maintain it.

After divorcing the husband she did not choose and embarking on a process of re-inventing herself, Sarah found that commitment had unexpectedly become an issue in her life. Most important is the reticence of many American men to commit to their partners, something I have found to be true as well. After presenting Sarah's story, I discuss some theories relevant to the issue of commitment. First are theories that contrast male and female socialization that have implications for why men tend to be commitment averse. Next I discuss psychoanalytic theories that explore pathologies of commitment, viz. people who over-commit, commit too easily, or who are unable to commit. Then I present clinical case studies that demonstrate commitments gone awry.

A chapter on Loyalty follows the chapter on commitment. After loyalty, the chapters take a dark turn and cover the following topics: Lying, Aggression, Envy, Revenge, Hate, and Evil. This Pandora's box of topics is examined with respect to pathologies associated with them and how commitment is undermined by these phenomena and the pathologies associated with them. The final three chapters cover Empathy, Forgiveness, and Mourning, all factors necessary to maintain commitments or repair betrayed loyalties. In order to elucidate these issues, every chapter concludes with at least two clinical cases.

It will perhaps become obvious that I wrote this book to explore the issues surrounding "love marriages" (my term for non-arranged marriages). I did not intend to write about hate, evil, etc., but these topics emerged organically from the writing process. In the course of my life experience as well as my psychiatric practice, I have repeatedly encountered these phenomena. They are germane to the topic of marriage because they can destroy a marriage.

CHAPTER 1

The Pakistani Patient

Empathy for a Fellow Immigrant

I n early 2015, I was contacted by "Sarah" who was interested in weekly psychotherapy and said she was having episodes of anxiety. She had been in therapy before. When asked, she said that she chose me because of my work writing Forensic Immigration Reports and because in my online photo (on my professional website, where she also saw my resume) I looked East Asian. Sarah is from Pakistan, and hoped that I was also an immigrant or, if not, that I would at least be better able to understand her experiences with the process of immigration.

My ability to empathize with Sarah was deepened by the fact that we both were in arranged marriages, and we both are now divorced. There was an immediate mutual identification between us.

The political hostility that exists between the nations of India and Pakistan is well known, but this did not affect our interaction. I am an immigrant from India with a long-standing interest in Pakistani culture (I speak Urdu) and I am aware of the similarities between Pakistani and Indian culture.

I have been treating Sarah for two years, seeing her two or three times a week in analytically oriented psychotherapy. Sarah has overcome many adversities in her life, she is highly intelligent, and her thought processes are clear and goal oriented. Sarah had witnessed a great deal of domestic violence growing up.

Sarah had a neurotic personality structure and was using repression-based defense mechanisms.

In other words, she was experiencing anxiety-laden thoughts but repressing it into her unconscious, preventing it from entering her conscious awareness. Sarah's repression was healthy and protective to her psyche because her anxiety would inhibit her ability to effectively deal with her environment. In addition, she had shown great resilience in her life, which—all else being equal—is a good indication that a person will benefit from analytically oriented psychotherapy. Sarah also displayed an ability to work in transference and to see the "as if" quality of the transference. In other words, Sarah was aware of the thoughts and emotions that she was projecting onto the analyst (i.e. transference), and was also aware that these projections had to do with her own unconscious thoughts and feelings as well as her past life experience (i.e. the "as if" quality of transference). She also had self-reflective capacity. Finally, her ego strengths were good, and her reality testing was intact.

Our shared experiences as immigrants and divorcees from arranged marriages presented me with a unique challenge as a therapist. Sarah and I would surely exhibit scotoma or blind spots regarding our shared experiences. If not recognized, these blind spots would interfere with treatment. This means that when discussing shared experiences, either the patient or therapist will assume they know what the other is talking or thinking about when in reality they do not. The result is that the treatment will be affected and will not go as deep as possible and the patient will not benefit fully from treatment. This can be prevented if the therapist is aware that scotoma are likely to occur, and if the therapist continually explores what those mean for the patient, rather than assuming that we know because we are from similar cultures. Again, given our similar backgrounds, I would need to be particularly careful not to make assumptions about Sarah's experiences.

Sarah's Background: Patriarchy and Violence

Sarah was born into a Muslim family in Pakistan, the youngest of nine children. Sarah has four brothers and four sisters. Her home life was replete with domestic violence (where women were always the victims) and misogyny: indeed, her nation is one of the world's most patriarchal, especially in rural areas. These factors, combined with fragments of American popular culture that filtered into Pakistani society, led Sarah to decide at age 13 that she would immigrate to the United States. American television fueled this dream, a dream so strong that she bought two posters of American kids and pretended that they were her kids. One poster was of a boy, the other of a girl. The girl had blonde hair and blue eyes.

Eventually, Sarah would realize her dream and would come to America.

Sarah's parents were role models for misogynistic domestic violence. Sarah characterized her mother as cognitively impaired, speculating that it may have be an effect of the physical and verbal abuse suffered at the hands of Sarah's father because he hit her hard and often. All four of Sarah's sisters suffered verbal abuse, and three of the four suffered physical abuse. Sarah's next oldest sibling, a sister, has perhaps endured the worst violence of any of Sarah's siblings. In one instance she was held down by her mother-in-law and brother-in-law so that her husband could punch and kick her. Sarah's sister divorced her husband, something only granted in cases of egregious violence. Unfortunately for Sarah's sister, in Pakistan (as in rural India) there is a stigma to being a divorced woman. There is no such stigma for men.

In contrast, none of Sarah's four brothers has ever been the victim of domestic violence. Two of the four had love marriages instead of arranged marriages. Sarah said that rural Pakistan is much different than Pakistan's large cities, and both of these brothers had moved to large cities before choosing to have non-arranged marriages. One of these brothers later moved to the U.S.

Coming to America

Sarah was an excellent student and earned a full scholarship to university and graduate school. After completing her degree, it was time to go to the United States. Sarah never deviated from this goal, though her journey would ultimately require great strength of purpose and some creative maneuvers through various bureaucracies.

Sarah arrived in the U.S.in 2002 with a six month visa. She travelled to the city where her brother was living. Despite arriving with impressive credentials in her field, Sarah enrolled in college at a level she had long ago exceeded. It was also the least expensive college in the city. The reason was simple: once enrolled, she was granted a three-year student visa.

Sarah was wearing the hijab in 2007, though she stopped wearing it later that year. She was still a traditional Muslim woman from rural Pakistan. She had an advanced degree and had shown herself to be resourceful and resolute in coming to and staying in the U.S. But she found the idea of freely choosing a husband too foreign. All of her siblings back in Pakistan (except for one brother) were in arranged marriages. At this point in her life, Sarah says she could not imagine anything other than an arranged marriage. So, Sarah entered into one too.

The marriage was arranged by Sarah's brother and happened in 2007. In Sarah's eyes, the match was doomed from the start. The groom, "Veejay," was six years older than Sarah and had been married previously. In addition, he was uneducated and not very intelligent. Veejay had a very low income, whereas Sarah intended to work in the U.S., and once she began working in her field would make far more money than Veejay. But most important was the fact they had nothing in common- except their daughter. Sarah had become pregnant on their wedding night or shortly thereafter.

The marriage lasted four months. In 2008, Sarah and Veejay were living under the same roof for the first time. She found him to be insufferably ignorant. Sarah did not want to live her life with this person. Sarah got a job in New York City and left, taking their young daughter with her.

Shortly after starting her new job, Sarah received a deportation order from the U.S. government. Veejay had gone to the immigration authorities—without Sarah's knowledge—and said he and Sarah had a "fraudulent marriage," that Sarah had married him in order to obtain a green card. Veejay was not a U.S. citizen at the time, and the rules surrounding marriage and green cards made his argument absurd. Nevertheless, Sarah had to hire an immigration attorney who turned the deportation order into citizenship for Sarah, obtaining citizenship for her through a "hardship waiver," meaning she would face physical violence if she returned to Pakistan.

Veejay then filed for custody of their daughter. The outcome was not favorable to him, however, and Sarah was granted sole custody and Veejay was required to pay child support.

Becoming American

Sarah's divorce from Veejay and everything that accompanied it had the effect of alienating her from her Muslim identity. Her alienation from Islam developed slowly at first, then accelerated until it reached a tipping point in 2015 when she rejected it entirely.

Such a change would be difficult for anyone and Sarah was no exception. Few people reject their religious heritage without experiencing trauma of some kind, either psychological, physical, or both. Sarah's fight with her ex-husband over her status as an immigrant and over custody of their daughter provided this trauma. On one hand was the legal fight in American courts, which Sarah won—after expending much time, effort, and money. On the other was the battle with the institutions of Shiite Islam, which was more decisive in Sarah's abandonment of her religion (but not her spirituality).

Under Islamic law, a woman can only divorce her husband with the permission of an Imam, and permission is usually granted only in cases of egregious physical abuse. The institutions of Islam (both Shiite and Sunni) are more decentralized than in any form of Christianity— Catholic, Protestant, or otherwise. Thus, any Imam could have granted Sarah a divorce from Veejay, but she was unable to find an Imam in the United States who was willing to do so. Ultimately, she found an Imam in Iran who was willing to nullify the marriage. A man from her hometown was studying Islam in Iran, and through him Sarah was able to obtain a divorce. It took Sarah four years to get a religious divorce from Veejay.

The issue that proved to be the greater catalyst for Sarah's abandonment of Islam was custody of her daughter. After a divorce, Islamic law stipulates that the husband gets full custody of the children. Sarah had already been granted joint custody of her daughter by an American court, but if she was to remain a "good Muslim" she would have to obey Islamic law and give her ex-husband full custody of their daughter. Sarah had fought hard for custody of her daughter and there was no way she was going to give her up, especially for a religion from which she was increasingly alienated.

During this time—2009 to 2014—Sarah was successful professionally, while simultaneously feeling psychologically "lost." She was living alone with her daughter (when she was not with her ex-husband), both wanting and not wanting to be in a relationship. While the immigration and custody battles played out, she struggled with anxiety and panic attacks. She did not have any sexual relations with men during this time, and was wrestling with her religious identity. She says that she did not feel lonely, but did feel a sense of longing. She could not, however, name what she was longing for.

Recognition as a Person

In 2012 she was at work when she felt a pain in her abdomen that she had never felt before. Priding herself on her independence, she did not tell anyone about it. But as the day progressed, the pain worsened. Eventually she drove herself to the hospital and was told that she had appendicitis and needed to have her appendix removed. She had surgery to remove her appendix and was in the hospital less than 48 hours.

According to Sarah, Dr. Feldman, a psychologist who worked at her place of business became interested in her because she had driven herself to the hospital while she was in a great deal of pain. Sarah says that it was the first time anyone had taken an interest in her for something other than instrumental reasons. It was the first time someone else was interested in her as a person. This would prove to be a pivotal experience in Sarah's life.

Dr. Feldman's interest in and concern for Sarah left her nonplussed. Not long after beginning therapy with Feldman, Sarah travelled to Pakistan to visit her family. Before she left, Dr. Feldman said, "I'll be thinking of you." Sarah says the first thought that came to her mind was, "Why would someone I hardly know care about my well-being?" This began a train of thought that ended with Sarah wondering why she was alone and deciding that it was time to start looking for a partner. So Sarah went looking for a mate in the most easily accessible place she knew: the internet.

Sarah began by looking on a "dating" site for Shiite Muslims from Pakistan. There she found uneducated men looking for women who would wear the hijab and be compliant, Muslim wives. She quickly moved on.

Two things happened during this period in Sarah's life. First, she started to look at men as individuals, as people, as opposed to potential husbands in arranged marriages that were little more than a collection of traits. Second, she shed her vestigial connection to Islam. Sarah put both feet outside the Mosque.

She left Islam for good when, in 2015, she was fasting for Ramadan "out of habit." One day she was hungry, she had a headache, and her daughter was acting up. Once her daughter settled down, Sarah fell asleep, woke up, and wondered why on earth she was observing Ramadan, one of Islam's most important holidays. Suddenly, it made no sense to her. Her head hurt and she was hungry. She stopped fasting and had something to eat. Shortly thereafter she renounced her Muslim faith and identity, though she is quick to point out that she is still "spiritual" and believes in god. But she has no use for Islam, and does not want people to know that she ever was a Muslim. Not because of the current political climate in the U.S. (which would be reason enough), but as a way of claiming and defining her identity for herself.

The Roots of Sarah's Resilience

According to Kernberg the development of "basic trust" is crucial to the normal development of the individual (Kernberg 2012, 277). This is usually provided by an individual's parents, but this was not the case for Sarah. By the time Sarah was born, her mother had "checked out" in every way except her physical presence. She was unavailable emotionally and unable to provide Sarah with any guidance or even care. As Sarah was to learn later, her mother did not want her and tried to abort her when she was pregnant. (She drank some sort of "medicine," which fortunately did not work.) Sarah's mother did virtually nothing for all of Sarah's childhood. Sarah says that she was a completely exhausted and spent human being. No sense of "basic trust" was forthcoming from Sarah's mother.

The same was true of Sarah's father, who was busy with the family business and had no time for Sarah's upbringing. Fortunately, Sarah gained a sense of basic trust from her siblings. This included a basic trust of arranged marriages, which helps explain why after two years in the U.S. she could not envision a non-arranged marriage. She was also living with her brother and sister-in-law during this time, which may also help explain her aversion to choosing her own partner. It was this brother who chose Sarah's husband and arranged the marriage.

Kernberg, in this theory of "Mature Love," points to the importance of marriage partners having an interest in the "life project" of their mate. Kernberg was talking of love marriages, not arranged marriages, but this concept is applicable to the latter. Sarah met her husband-to-be exactly once before they were married. She had no idea who he was. To her dismay, he was completely incompatible with her. He was poorly educated, not very intelligent, and very insecure. Sarah had no interest in her husband's life project; he was "too different."

During the four months that Sarah and Veejay lived together, his insecurity about their relationship manifested constantly. He would speak about her earning potential vs. his and would say things like, "you are going to leave me once you start making money." This proved to be true, as Sarah left him well before then. Sometimes, fears and insecurities are not unfounded.

Winnicott argued that the greater a person's capacity for being alone, the greater his capacity to have a meaningful relationship with another person and the less he will fear abandonment (Winnicott 1958). In addition, the greater a person's tolerance for being alone, the greater his ability to tolerate "disillusionment in love" (Winnicott 1960). Having parents who were for all intents and purposes absent, Sarah experienced aloneness throughout her childhood. This made her accustomed to being alone and, thus, unafraid of being abandoned. It also prepared her for the failure of her marriage.

Her marriage to Veejay and all the troubles that came with it fundamentally changed Sarah. When she got married, she was still a traditional Pakistani Muslim, unable to picture herself choosing her own husband, still wearing the hijab. After four months with Veejay, her divorce, a move across the country, Veejay's attempt to have her deported, the custody battle, and the struggle to get their marriage annulled by a Muslim cleric, Sarah no longer identified as a Muslim. She also became interested in men without male relatives acting as intermediaries, thoughts and actions taboo in rural Pakistan.

Sarah's Continuing Self-Definition

When Sarah came to me for treatment in early 2015, she was struggling to create an identity from a mixture of two very different cultures: traditional, rural Pakistan and its cultural practices like arranged marriages, and the dizzying, fragmented array of beliefs and practices that constitute American "culture." I had gone through a similar experience of creating a stable sense of self some years earlier. This was another shared aspect of our respective experiences that made it possible for us to connect on a deeper level than if she had gone into psychotherapy with an American psychiatrist.

Sarah grew to trust and confide in me as part of therapeutic alliance. She began sharing her inner life. She had been in therapy before with Dr.

Feldman, but this therapeutic relationship did not end well. Increasingly dissatisfied, Sarah terminated her relationship with Feldman but remained interested in pursuing psychotherapy.

More than ever, Sarah was thriving professionally but still feeling lost psychologically. She had shed all vestiges of her Muslim identity. This was an easy change to make compared to her ongoing project of self-definition. In addition, for the first time in her life Sarah was dating. This was proving to be the most difficult aspect of Sarah's identity creation. She was meeting plenty of men on the dating websites where she had posted profiles but was frustrated by her experiences. What frustrated her most was the unwillingness of American men to commit.

Nostalgia

Commitment—or the lack thereof—became a main theme of sessions with Sarah. Although she was enjoying the freedom of dating, she was nostalgic for aspects of arranged marriages. Specifically, she wished— on a primordial level—that someone or something would choose a mate for her and together they would settle into a happy domestic life. Sarah knew, of course, that this was an unrealistic fantasy born of her frustrations in dating, primarily her inability to find a compatible mate who was willing to commit to her. Akhtar refers to this as an "as if fantasy," viz. an unrealistic fantasy the immigrant has related to his country of origin (Akhtar 1996). For all its faults, an arranged marriage would provide both a partner and commitment without any effort on Sarah's part.

CHAPTER 2
A Love Marriage Template

After working with Sarah for a few weeks, I decided that she would benefit from analytically oriented psychotherapy, in particular regarding her approach to relationships. She first came to me for therapy after her divorce, and I could see that she was having difficulty forming and maintaining healthy relationships. The thought of Otto Kernberg and his ideas on what constitutes "Mature Love" came to mind (Kernberg 2012).

The first of these is "interest in the life project of the other." Sarah was unable to develop this with her husband because the two of them were so different. Arranged marriages are not well-suited for the development of a deep interest in the life of the other. Sarah met her husband-to-be once before they were married. This is hardly enough time to develop an interest in the other's life project. In arranged marriages, the development of this aspect of mature love is essentially left to chance. This is in stark contrast to love marriages, where prospective partners are able to decide for themselves whether they are this interested in the other's life project.

The second aspect of Kernberg's Mature Love is "basic trust," defined as feeling comfortable enough with the other to share one's most intimate thoughts, feelings, vulnerabilities, and needs. Basic trust is an implicit trust that one's partner will accept these aspects of one's inner life without judgment. Thus, both partners can give voice to their inner lives without fear that doing so will jeopardize the relationship.

The third aspect of Mature Love is the capacity for "authentic forgiveness." This is the ability to both ask for forgiveness and to forgive the behavior of others. It applies not only to the partners in the relationship, but more broadly to others in society. Feelings of aggression are natural in relationship conflicts, and the ability to let this aggression fade and resume normal interaction is a major component of Mature Love.

The fourth aspect of Mature Love is "humility and gratitude." Humility is a general orientation toward the other and the world, recognizing that nobody is right all the time and having the confidence and self-esteem to admit when one is wrong. Gratitude is a deeply felt thankfulness for the existence of the other person and the love he gives. In addition, with humility and gratitude one accepts dependence on the other person and the inevitable struggles and conflicts inherent in life.

As with interest in the other's life project, the other aspects of Kernberg's Mature Love are problematic in the context of an arranged marriage. This is not to say that achieving them is impossible, but for this to happen a basic compatibility and set of shared interests has to exist. Whether the marriage partners have this similarity is, again, largely a matter of chance. Kernberg developed his notion of Mature Love to apply to love marriages where partners come together of their own free will, not to arranged marriages where family members decide who one's partner will be.

Kernberg's Mature Love, therefore, is a model for Sarah to emulate as she adapts to the new cultural norm of romantic love and the search for a partner.

CHAPTER 3

Choosing Commitment

Freedom is not the absence of commitments, but the ability to choose- and commit myself to- what is best for me.

—Paulo Coelho

could understand Sarah's "as if" fantasies regarding arranged marriages because I, too, once had such fantasies. After all, in an arranged marriage, the bride-to-be is completely passive. Ignoring the myriad negative aspects of arranged marriages—as Sarah was during her nostalgic "as if" fantasies—she was free of the burden of finding a partner. All aspects of commitment—physical, emotional, and otherwise—were taken care of by others. The reality, of course, is quite different, and Sarah gradually became aware of this. It was necessary, however, for us to work through her fantasies and understand them.

Both of us were well aware of how far Sarah's fantasies were from the realities of arranged marriage. If a woman is lucky, she will be paired with a man who is a good match. But even a "good match" exists in the context of extreme patriarchy. The husband and his extended family have all the power. The price of passivity is vulnerability to the whims of men, which manifest themselves in domestic violence with depressing regularity.

The institution of arranged marriage is patriarchal in every way. Men can easily divorce their wives, while divorce for a woman is quite difficult. It is usually not granted except in cases of extreme domestic violence. And even if a woman succeeds in obtaining a divorce, she bears a stigma so powerful that no man will marry her. Men, of course, face no such post-divorce stigma. In short, in an arranged marriage the woman is little more than property.

Sarah entertained her "as-if" fantasies for a relatively short period of time. She was too aware of the reality of arranged marriage to continue her fantasies for very long. Thus, her fantasies were short-lived and were not a problem. The very real problem was dating and the problem of finding a man willing to commit to a serious relationship. This issue came up repeatedly in Sarah's treatment, and I found myself wondering why American men seem so commitment-averse. Helping Sarah work though her idealized fantasies about arranged marriages was relatively easy, but over time I found myself becoming frustrated at Sarah's predicament. I was not frustrated with Sarah, but with the reality with which she was wrestling.

Over the years I had my own issues with commitment and had given it much thought. As Sarah recounted her struggles, her words brought up strong feelings, and I found myself struggling to maintain my objectivity. I managed to remain aware of my countertransference without offering advice or sharing my opinions on commitment. I worked through my countertransference and kept my opinions to myself, using them to further understand Sarah.

Socialization and Gender Roles

Little has been written specifically about commitment in psychiatry or other social sciences, but much has been written about related issues that sheds light on the topic. The most important of these is socialization into male and female gender roles. It stands to reason that the way males and females are taught to regard members of the opposite sex will reveal why some people—men in particular—are so commitment averse.

In all societies, males and females learn different lessons about who they are, how they should behave, and their relative standing in society. The formal education of the sexes appears to be the same, but more important lessons about what constitutes appropriate behavior for the sexes are learned informally and unconsciously. These lessons are learned from parents, relatives, peers, and popular culture, and teach males and females very different behaviors and ways of thinking. From the moment they enter this world, boys and girls are socialized into different gender roles.

Nancy Chodorow argues that differences in parenting are responsible for differential gender socialization and thus different gender roles (Chodorow 1978). Boys are taught to separate from their mothers sooner than girls and to mimic the behavior of their fathers, perpetuating a distinctly male culture. This culture is characterized by aggressive behavior, competition, and machismo. In contrast, girls stay emotionally connected to their mothers for a longer period of time. They are socialized into a distinctly female culture where the emphasis is on cooperation and emotional connection.

Deborah Tannen has shown that American males and females are socialized to have markedly different communication styles (Tannen 1992). They are, however, largely unaware of these differences; the result is that ordinary communication between the sexes frequently leads to conflict. When women communicate with men, they expect a response in accordance with how they were socialized; the converse is true when men communicate with women. Tannen argues this differential socialization does not occur just in the home but everywhere, all the time. Prior to adolescence, boys and girls inhabit separate social worlds. They learn together in the same classrooms, but otherwise remain quite segregated, far more than is generally recognized. The result is socialization into distinctly male and female cultures with different styles of communication.

Different communication styles, however, are not the most important lesson learned through gender socialization. That distinction goes to the sexual double-standard, ubiquitous in American society yet not consciously recognized by mainstream culture. In short, the sexual double standard means that promiscuous males are judged differently than promiscuous females. Contrary to various "official" moral worldviews that preach the virtues of monogamy, promiscuous males are following a widely accepted social norm and are rewarded in various ways. There is no equivalent "unofficial" norm for women, and promiscuous females are vilified. This is reflected in the English language itself; there are many derogatory words for a woman who "sleeps around," but no equivalent words for promiscuous men. A female who sleeps around is a slut, a whore, etc. A male who sleeps around is described as a "stud" or with some equally positive adjective. The double standard has lessened somewhat in recent years, but contrary to popular belief it is still alive and well, including on college campuses (Allison and Risman 2014).

The double-standard does not explain the difference between men and women with respect to commitment, but it does suggest an answer. The double-standard plays a key role in men and women's different attitudes towards commitment. A subterranean norm for men that glorifies sexual conquest is unlikely to co-exist with a desire for commitment. The same is true for the elements of male socialization that emphasize individualism and autonomy, and foster a disdain for emotional or any other type of dependence on another person. In addition, there are also theories which claim a role for biology. The basic argument is that gender roles are "hard-wired" into human biology. Even a cursory knowledge of the vast array of gender roles across cultures and throughout history disproves crude biological determinism. This does not mean, however, that biology plays no role in shaping gender roles. It quite likely does, though it interacts with culture to produce the gender roles we observe.

The Love Object

There are also a number of psychoanalytic theories that explain why people suffer from a fear of abandonment, leading to a reluctance to commit. Fears of abandonment can manifest in either pathological or non-pathological forms.

Attachment Theory posits that the formation of "secure attachments" are necessary for healthy psychological development (Winnicott 1957). A secure attachment occurs when a child develops a stable, reliable bond with his primary caregiver. This bond is created when the caregiver is responsive to the child's needs, provides protection, and the child knows that he can depend on the caregiver to return. Individuals who form a secure attachment are unlikely—all else being equal—to develop pathology.

Failure to develop a secure attachment will, however, result in one of three types of pathology, depending on the nature of the relationship between the child and his primary caregiver. Two of these insecure attachments may result in a fear of abandonment. In the first of these, the children are insecure and anxious about their relationships. They tend to have low self-esteem, feel less positive about their relationships (romantic and otherwise), are less trusting of their partners, and thus they fear being abandoned by their love object. The second insecure attachment pathology produces individuals who are highly ambivalent about their relationships, both wanting and not wanting emotional closeness. These individuals find it difficult to trust those with whom they have relationships, making them prone to fearing abandonment by them. The third possible outcome are individuals who do not, in general, fear abandonment. They are emotionally distant, view intimacy with distrust, and tend to have a low opinion of their relationship partners. The latter is especially true when their relationships end.

Margaret Mahler offers a different perspective on the fear of abandonment (Mahler 1985). Mahler argued that the most important aspect of psychological development is the formation of "object constancy." Object constancy is the developmental attainment that enables an individual to preserve a stable internal representation of an object, even in the face of complex or contradictory emotions experienced towards the object. It is established by age three. Piaget held a similar concept called object permanence (Piaget 1966). This is a strictly cognitive capacity to maintain a representation of an object (animate or inanimate) even when it is not in the child's perceptual awareness and is fully developed by 18 months.)

Extreme fear of abandonment is seen in individuals who suffer from Borderline Personality Disorder. Characteristics of borderline personality disorders include a fragmented identity (a.k.a. "identity disturbance"), an unstable self-image, and an impaired ability to interact normatively. They are subject to mood swings and can oscillate between idealizing and devaluing those close to them. In other words, they swing between love and hate. Individuals with borderline personalities are also prone to self-destructive behaviors such as addiction, self-mutilation, and suicide.

The Capacity to be Alone

The second factor that can explain an inability to commit is a limited capacity to be alone. Like Mahler and Piaget, Winnicott argues that the most important stage of a person's development is the formation of "object constancy" (Winnicott 1957). Winnicott, however, adds to the notion of object constancy the idea that there must be an "internalized good object." Winnicott's internalized good object is somewhat similar to Kernberg's notion of basic trust; not only is the caregiver's autonomy accepted, but with this acceptance comes a feeling that the world is essentially a good place. This gives the child the confidence he will need to deal with the travails of life.

The benefits of this development are great, as are the drawbacks should the "good object" fail to form. Winnicott argues that this feeling of basic goodness is necessary for emotional maturity and for understanding oneself and one's inner life. More importantly, the feeling of basic goodness is a necessary condition for being alone without being lonely. For Winnicott, with this defense in place, one has a strong enough sense of self to avoid feeling lonely when alone, even if one is alone for a substantial period of time.

Conversely, Winnicott maintains that failure to develop the internalized good object does not necessarily result in pathology, but it will have a profound effect on the person's life. For example, children who have been traumatized by physical, emotional, and/or sexual abuse will have difficulty forming this sense of goodness. This, in turn, leads to an inability to form relationships. In a cruel irony, children who are rejected violently by their caregivers are affected in a way that makes healthy connection with others difficult. In a further irony, these people who are unable to form relationships are also unable to tolerate aloneness.

Optimal Psychic Space

The importance of establishing an "optimal psychic space" has been argued by Salman Akhtar (Akhtar 1999). He defines it as "[A] psychic position that permits intimacy without loss of autonomy and separateness and without painful aloneness." Obviously this is an ideal unlikely to be realized by anyone one hundred percent of the time, and Akhtar recognizes that maintaining optimal psychic space is a continual struggle and a goal that never can be fully achieved.

No two people will always desire the same degree of space, and judging the proper space between oneself and the love object is difficult. For some people, however, it is nearly impossible. Their inability to render accurate judgments about optimal space has its roots in childhood. If the primary caregiver was not optimally available, the child's development will be arrested. The result is that the child fails to develop a sense for creating optimal distance. A number of pathologies can result from this situation.

First is the development of a person with a borderline personality disorder. Again, borderline personalities are characterized by a fragmented identity, self-destructive behaviors, and a deep ambivalence for the love object. The latter is the most important pathology with respect to maintaining optimal space. A person who oscillates between utter infatuation with the love object and hatred of it is unlikely to maintain optimal psychic space.

Second is the development of the narcissistic personality disorder. People with narcissistic personality disorders are incapable of true intimacy. They are so focused on themselves that they devalue others and simply do not see the value in trusting anyone. They also frequently lack empathy, a personality trait necessary for accepting the imperfections of the love object.

Last is the schizoid personality, a severe personality disorder that results in a complete withdrawal from society. People with schizoid personalities live in a fantasy world, leaving them incapable of dealing with the real world, let alone judging the "optimal space" between themselves and others.

Basic Trust

According to Erik Erikson, a child's sense of trust develops during the first year of life (Erikson 1950). The basis for this trust is the presence of the caregiver and their responsiveness to the infant's needs. If the caregiver consistently responds to the child's needs, the result is a normal level of trust. If, however, the caregiver is absent and/or unresponsive when the child is in need, trust will fail to develop. As an adult, the person will find trusting others difficult and will therefore have difficulty committing to another person.

Furthermore, a person who has been betrayed will be reluctant to trust again. This is especially true if that person has exposed their inner life in confidence and had this confidence broken. Betrayal and/or dishonesty by others makes distrustfulness a rational choice. People who experience other people as consistently untrustworthy have little reason to trust anyone, drop their guard and reveal their vulnerabilities.

Loss of Freedom

Fear of losing one's freedom by committing exclusively to another person cannot reasonably be called a pathology. Rather, it is a personal choice shaped by how one defines freedom. To use economic terms, it is a choice that entails costs and benefits. The benefits of commitment include a sense of purpose, companionship, someone with whom one can share one's interests, etc. A possible cost of monogamous commitment is that one becomes trapped in an unfulfilling relationship. The cost of commitment is the loss of freedom to have other relationships, whereas a typical cost of freedom is loneliness.

The fear of losing one's freedom is not, however, associated with pathology. It depends on one's value system and is a personal choice.

CLINICAL CASES

Patients come to therapy presenting a variety of symptoms: depression, anxiety, compulsions, phobias, etc. I usually begin by exploring the possible hereditary, environmental, and psychological causes of their complaints. I find that many of the problems patients are experiencing are caused by their difficulties in relationships. The psychological characteristics and/or social contexts of these patients make it difficult if not impossible for them to maintain a committed relationship.

Amy

Amy is a successful saleswoman, but her professional success obscures serious psychological problems that interfere with her ability to form and maintain committed relationships. Amy is extremely insecure and has a fragmented sense of self. These and other factors combine to make Amy prone to codependent behavior.

Amy's codependence presented itself in full when she caught her boyfriend cheating. She had been suspicious for a few months, and her suspicions were confirmed when she looked in his phone and found that he had been calling and texting another woman. The content of the texts made it clear that he was cheating.

Amy responded to what she saw as the loss of her boyfriend's love with extreme possessiveness. Consistent with her codependent tendencies, Amy did not break up with him but became even more clingy. This did not, however, draw him closer to her. The more possessive Amy became, the more her boyfriend withdrew from her emotionally and physically. One Friday night he went out with his friends and she demanded that he text her every half hour. He agreed, then disappeared for the entire weekend, saying that he spent it at a friend's beach house.

Amy assumed that he had cheated on her. He finally had enough and left; Amy subsequently fell apart psychologically.

Amy's psychological profile made her collapse all but inevitable. Her codependence makes her unable to give the people she loves adequate physical and psychic space. Her inability to negotiate an optimal space between herself and others is most evident in her romantic relationships. Amy has little tolerance for being alone, which is frequently a characteristic of people prone to codependent behavior.

I tried to make Amy aware of her behavior patterns. Codependent people form romantic relationships easily, attach themselves tightly to the love object, and believe themselves to be deeply in love. This pattern is rather predictable, and for every codependent person there is a large population of people with whom they could (theoretically) form an attachment.

My primary task was to get Amy to recognize her codependent behavior patterns. The first time I tried this, Amy was very resistant. She was resistant to talk about it. Eventually she became more receptive to talking about it. Slowly she got to the point where she was willing to acknowledge the fundamental behavior pattern of codependence: the propensity to attach too tightly to the love object because of the fear of losing it.

In general, I try to make patients aware of the motives and meanings behind their behavior. Amy's codependence was tied to her traumatic past. Her family history was replete with alcoholism and mood disorders, and Amy had engaged in various self-destructive behaviors when she was younger. Her codependence was largely a product of her past.

Long-lasting behavioral patterns take time to change, and the patient must be willing to try. Amy is just beginning to recognize her maladaptive behavior patterns and the ways in which they hurt her. Fortunately, she is having gradual insight in to her behavior matters and together we are gradually working to further Amy's self-awareness.

Karl

The following case is of a couple whose commitment to each other has been severely tested by an extraneous event. As a result, their marriage has been transformed from one where commitment came relatively easily to one where maintaining commitment is a daily struggle.

Karl is a stock broker in his mid-30s who is married to a high school teacher. The couple has one child and Karl's wife is pregnant with a second. When Karl's first child was six months old, he was diagnosed with lissencephaly, a genetic brain disorder that causes emotional problems, cognitive impairment, and seizures. When Karl heard his son's diagnosis, he became anxious about the fate of his second child. He worried obsessively that the baby his wife was carrying would suffer from the same disease as his son.

His son's illness challenged the solidity of Karl's marriage and his commitment to his wife. Karl's son suffered from frequent seizures and required constant attention. Karl and his wife decided that she would quit her job and stay home to care for the child. Before long, Karl felt that his wife resented him for what he thought was a mutual decision. To support his family, Karl began working overtime. The pressures of work and home, however, caused him to feel burned out and depressed. He began avoiding home, instead spending his limited free time with friends and lying to his wife about where he had been. Not surprisingly, his wife became suspicious and angry, feeling that Karl's avoidance behavior was placing an extra burden on her.

The more Karl lied and avoided home, the more his wife resented him. Karl and his wife wound up in a vicious cycle of deception, resentment, and distrust. They are both under a great deal of stress and have little time for themselves or each other. Intimacy has become almost impossible in this context, and Karl has lost interest in his wife sexually. All of this has severely strained Karl's marriage and his commitment to his wife.

The primary stressor in this case is the constant care required by Karl's son. It struck Karl and his wife without warning like a bolt of lightening, for all intents and purposes occurring extraneous to their marriage. Neither Karl nor his wife exhibited any pathology, and their marriage was free of any significant pathology. The couples' behavior did not change, but an external force suddenly put enormous pressure on their commitment to each other. After all, Karl only sought treatment after his son's diagnosis.

In this case the primary cause of the problem was not individual pathology but an external event, one that disrupted the established professional and domestic roles of Karl and his wife, dramatically increasing their stress levels and workloads. They have adapted to their situation, but it is unlikely that this adaptation can continue indefinitely. Unfortunately they are unable to afford full-time care for their son, so elements of their adaptation are likely to remain as they are.

I suggested that Karl enlist the help of his extended family in caring for his son. He would then be able to spend time with his wife and re-establish some intimacy. In addition, I tried to help Karl come to terms with his new set of roles and responsibilities. For this to happen, he has to mourn his old roles and responsibilities. Karl has a long journey ahead of him as he mourns his old identity and adapts to his new circumstances.

A CHOICE CONTINUALLY RENEWED

The above cases demonstrate the challenges of commitment in relationships and marriage. In the first case, one person's psychopathology—codependence—led to the dissolution of the relationship. Relationships and marriages where both parties suffer from psychopathology provide an even less stable basis for the union. In the second case, an event extraneous to the marriage has severely stressed the spouses' commitment to each other. Unlike an arranged marriage in a traditional society, there is little that holds love marriages together apart from the continual effort of both individuals to renew their commitment.

CHAPTER 4

Loyalty and Betrayal

He that has eyes to see and ears to hear may convince himself that no mortal can keep a secret. If his lips are silent, he chatters with his fingertips; betrayal oozes out of him at every pore.

—Sigmund Freud

We cannot examine the issue of commitment without examining the issue of loyalty. The two are inextricably intertwined; one cannot keep a commitment without remaining loyal to the goals of that commitment. A husband takes wedding vows to remain faithful to his wife, and vice versa. This is considered a sacred vow, a commitment. To remain faithful is to be loyal, but if someone cheats then the commitment is broken and someone has been betrayed. We cannot examine loyalty without examining betrayal—the breaking of a commitment.

The *Merriam-Webster Dictionary* online defines loyalty as follows:

1. faithful to a private person to whom fidelity is due
2. faithful in allegiance to one's lawful sovereign or government
3. faithful to a cause, ideal, custom, institution, or product

The first definition is, obviously, the most relevant to the discussion of relationships. Other types of loyalty, however, can also play a role in relationships because people feel an attachment to various institutions, causes, etc. These sometimes conflict with a person's loyalty to another person.

Personality Disorders

Two personality disorders make people prone to betrayal, and one makes a person more likely to be a victim of betrayal. The first is narcissistic personality disorder; the personality characteristics of this disorder combine in ways that compel individuals to break loyalties and betray other people. The most important aspect of narcissists relative to betrayal is their unwillingness and/or inability to recognize the feelings and needs of other people. Narcissists have a sense of entitlement and feel that the world owes them attention if not admiration, and they tend to be haughty and arrogant in their self-presentation. They expect other people to do their bidding regardless of their circumstances or prior commitments.

Narcissists are ruthless in their pursuits (the results of which they tend to exaggerate) and lack compassion for other people. According to Winnicott narcissists exhibit a significant split between their public personae and their "true self" (Winnicott 1971). Winnicott argues that if a narcissist feels that their true self has been revealed, they may go into a rage and engage in self- and other-destructive behaviors. In short, narcissists think only of themselves, have an exaggerated self-image, and are potentially dangerous should their self-presentation be exposed.

The second personality disorder associated with betrayal is antisocial personality disorder. In simple Freudian terms, these individuals are pure Id with weak Ego structures and an absent Superego. The latter is the defining characteristic of people with antisocial personalities: they have no conscience. Regardless of their actions, they are incapable of feeling remorse.

Feeling remorse is about the only thing they are incapable of. They engage in the full panoply of anti-social behaviors: they lie, cheat, steal, and manipulate others to get what they want. They are often impulsive and irresponsible, characteristics that are sometimes accompanied by aggressive and violent behavior. Their impulsiveness and aggression make these people prone to self-destructive behaviors like alcoholism and drug abuse.

The third pathology is self-defeating personality disorder (sometimes called masochistic personality disorder). People with this disorder are likely to be victims of betrayal. The constellation of personality traits predisposes these individuals to engage in self-defeating behaviors which often leave them vulnerable to people who take advantage of them. The DSM-5 provides the following summary of this personality disorder:

> Self-defeating Personality Disorder is a pervasive pattern of self-defeating behavior, beginning by early adulthood and present in a variety of contexts. The person may often avoid or undermine pleasurable experiences, be drawn to situations or relationships in which he or she will suffer, and prevent others from helping him or her (DSM-5 2013).

Self-defeaters greet personal accomplishments with feelings of failure, they reject help from others, they reject opportunities for pleasure, and they reject people who consistently treat them well. Their introversion and inward orientation makes them naïve and thus prone to betrayal by others.

Psychoanalysis and Personality Disorders

Severe narcissistic and anti-social personality disorders are not (in my opinion) amenable to psychoanalysis though other forms of therapy may be appropriate. People without a conscience or sense of remorse cannot benefit from analysis because of their fundamental dishonesty. The absence of guilt on their part puts the analyst in the impossible position of having to discern when patients are lying and when they are telling the truth; everything they say is suspect. Narcissists are grandiose and exaggerate their accomplishments, and anti-social personalities are likely to view analysis with contempt.

Self-defeating personalities can benefit from analysis because they have a conscience. The analyst can trust that their responses are honest, or at least what they believe to be honest.

Some patients benefit from analysis, while others are more likely to benefit from other types of psychotherapy. Whatever the method, my first role is to try to understand patients' behavior patterns and make them conscious of it. In most cases, patients will be entirely or partly unconscious of the patterns that they continue to act out. Making them aware of these patterns is the first step towards healing. Second, I try to get my patients to understand the motivations behind their behaviors. Once they understand their motivations, they can work to change them.

Salman Akhtar's Categories

In his book *Sources of Suffering*, Salman Akhtar creates his own categories for people prone to betrayal of others (Akhtar 2014). These are not diagnostic categories from the DSM-5, but the product of Akhtar's clinical observations. Akhtar does not have a category for people likely to be betrayed; all three of Akhtar's categories describe people who betray others. Unlike the disorders described above, there is no category equivalent to self-defeating personality disorder.

The first two types have relatively benign causes and motivations; the third evokes narcissistic and anti-social personality disorders.

Akhtar's describes people in his first category as having "diffuse ego impairment." These people lack a strong sense of self and are what some people call "people pleasers." They mean well, but they lack the strength of self to say "no," to refuse to do things for others that they neither have the time nor the ability to do. Thus, they wind up betraying others because they cannot follow through on their commitments.

The second of Akhtar's compulsive motivations are people who "over-identify with overpromising parents." These people grew up with parents who would make promises—sometimes grandiose promises—and then fail to honor them. Repeated disappointments over many years is traumatizing, and this trauma imprints itself on the personality of the child. As adults, these individuals come to identify with their parents, and unconsciously reenact their parents' behavior. They make promises they cannot keep and often outdo their parents in terms of betraying people. They are not conscious of their betrayals, often have the best of intentions, and are genuinely surprised to learn of the effects of their behavior on others.

The third of Akhtar's compulsive motivations he calls "sadistic triumph over envied others." This is the most serious and the most malevolent of the three personality types. Again, the cause is serious trauma involving some sort of betrayal during childhood, and these people become obsessively jealous and resentful of their siblings. As adults, they betray others with a "sadistic glee" that is a "combination of pathological self-absorption, cruelty and antisocial behavior." Their unrelenting jealousy and hatred of their siblings has been turned towards people in general.

CLINICAL CASES

Sarah

Sarah experienced her share of betrayal at the hands of the men in her life. She told me how her brother stole approximately $100,000 from an account in Pakistan that she had set up for her mother. Sarah has been supporting various members of her family for some years. She is still unclear how he managed to do it, but her brother (the one living in the U.S.)—who was experiencing financial problems—took the money without telling Sarah—and without returning it. Sarah confronted her brother but he was unable to repay it at the time, and she let it slide. She put the money back in her mother's account with clear instructions to the bank that only her mother had the authority to make withdrawals.

Sarah's experiences with her ex-husband were much worse. I have already discussed how Veejay tried to get Sarah deported after she ended their marriage. Considering that Sarah could potentially have been the target of violence if she had been returned to Pakistan, Veejay's actions could be considered a form of assault. It made me angrier than it seemed to make Sarah, who was angry with Veejay for a time but forgave him rather quickly.

During the period when Veejay tried to get Sarah deported, he also committed petty fraud against Sarah. First, he used her name and good credit (his was not good) to open a joint checking account. He did not, however, inform Sarah of this and she only found out when she saw a bank statement in the mail. A second betrayal of Sarah by Veejay was when he lost his job and began to receive unemployment insurance—and did not tell Sarah. Finally, Veejay filed a joint tax return, again without Sarah's knowledge. She found out when she received a letter from the IRS saying that she owed money—because Veejay had incorrectly filled out the form. Sarah was angry, but she decided upon the path of least resistance and paid the bill.

This seems to be a recurring pattern: Veejay does something terrible (unforgivable in the view of some), Sarah gets angry but then forgives him.

I can only speculate on the pathologies that compel Veejay to treat Sarah this way. Sarah thought that Veejay felt no guilt or remorse over his actions. Usually this would indicate some degree of sociopathy, but this diagnosis is complicated by cultural factors, most importantly the subservient role of women in Pakistan. If they were in Pakistan, Veejay's betrayals of Sarah would be the norm. At any rate, never having met Veejay (although having heard much about him) I was in no position to offer a professional opinion, neither was it my role to do it. As an immigrant from that part of the world, however, I can readily attest to the pervasive patriarchy there and how a man could feel no guilt treating a woman (even his own wife) this way.

Betty

The second case provides a particularly egregious example of betrayal. Betty is a 62 year old nurse who has been married to her husband for 25 years. Betty came to me when she found out that her husband had been having affairs for 15 years—with men. She had been suspicious for some time and finally confronted him. He easily, almost casually, confirmed her suspicions. Betty was doubly shocked: she learned that her husband of 25 years was not only having affairs, he was having them with men. Betty is not particularly homophobic, but her shock is understandable. For 25 years her husband gave no indication that he was having affairs or that he was attracted to men.

Betty's husband broke their commitment, was disloyal, and betrayed her in a dramatic way. She is currently married but separated from her husband and has initiated divorce proceedings.

Betty did not present symptoms of self-defeating personality disorder. That is, she does not possess the characteristics that make people susceptible to betrayal. Her husband, however, exhibits signs of narcissistic personality disorder. Assuming Betty accurately described his behavior, he showed no remorse—the hallmark of a narcissist.

Janet and Roger

I am also treating Janet and Roger in couples' therapy. Unlike Betty, Janet suffered betrayal with deadly consequences. Janet and Roger came to me after Roger had gone on one of his many business trips and Janet discovered that he had cheated on her. Roger, in fact, had been serially cheating on Janet. What's worse, Roger gave Janet HIV which he contracted on one of his "business trips." Janet gave the impression that Roger lacked any sense of guilt or remorse about either his cheating or giving her HIV.

Roger did not present symptoms of narcissistic personality disorder, but he did present anti-social personality traits. Janet displayed traits consistent with self-defeating personality disorder, most notably the fact that she remains in her relationship with Roger.

CHOOSING LOYALTY

Narcissists and anti-social personalities are not constrained by conscience; they feel no guilt or remorse betraying those close to them, including their spouses. Betrayal comes easy for those without moral restraint. For the rest of us, loyalty is like commitment—it is a choice that one continually needs to make.

CHAPTER 5
The Most Common Betrayal

The worst lies are the lies we tell ourselves. We live in denial of what we do, even what we think we do this because we are afraid.
—**Johann Sebastian Bach**

No treatment of marriage would be complete without a discussion of lying. Deceiving one's partner—and often the activities the deception facilitates—is one of the most frequent problems patients deal with in therapy. Regardless of the complaint they first present, conversation in therapy frequently turns to romantic relationships. The vast majority of the time deception plays a significant role in patients' relationship problems. The discovery that their partner has deceived them is frequently what brings them to treatment in the first place.

The *Merriam-Webster Dictionary* online defines a lie as follows: "1) a falsehood uttered or acted for the purpose of deception; 2) an intentional violation of truth; 3) an untruth spoken with the intention to deceive." An aspect of the normative order is to consider lying bad; children are admonished not to lie and always to tell the truth. Children quickly learn, of course, that nobody tells the truth all the time. We teach our children that uttering falsehoods, intentionally violating the truth, and intentionally deceiving others is wrong, but children can see that this is not true. They can see that the real world is replete with situations where telling the truth would have facilitated an evil much greater than lying.

For example, the heroic attempt to save Anne Frank's family from the Nazis was based on deception. The Frank family left Germany for the Netherlands, and went into hiding when the Nazis began to arrest Jews and send them to the death camps. When the Nazis asked if there were Jews hiding on the premises, the people hiding Anne and her family denied it. Of course, they were hiding Jews—a capital offense in Nazi Germany—but one is on shaky moral ground to argue that they should have told the Nazis the truth.

The specific reasons for lying are theoretically infinite, but they generally fit into a number of specific categories. They are as follows:

- to hide information
- for gain, financial or otherwise
- to hurt others
- to divert blame away from oneself

Less straightforward is the question of whether withholding relevant information is a lie. It is a type of deception to possess information that others want but to pretend not to have it. The same ethical principles, however, apply to this form of deception as to blatant lies. The people who harbored Anne Frank and her family were withholding information relevant to the Nazis' Final Solution, who wanted to register every Jew living in the Netherlands. Those who harbored the Frank family did not, however, go to Nazi headquarters and report that they were in fact hiding Jews. Withholding this information was a lie, but one justified by the evil of the Nazi regime.

The same ethical principles apply to keeping secrets, which is also a form of deception and which often involve blatant lying. As in withholding information, the ethics of keeping secrets depend on the nature of the secret itself, not the deception involved.

Lying to Oneself

Perhaps the most interesting and least understood lies are those we tell ourselves. The notion that one can lie to oneself raises a number of questions. For example, there are people who tell the same lie about themselves for a long period of time. The question arises, have they come to believe these lies and, if so, when did this happen? Or do they switch back and forth between believing what they say and knowing that it is not true? And if they are aware that they shift between lying and truthfulness, what do they feel? Do they feel guilty? If not, how should we characterize their personalities?

It is possible that some people are able to believe what they need to believe in a particular context, then believe something else in a different context. In different contexts the person believes different things. In other words, their beliefs change to meet the needs of the moment. People who are capable of this actually believe their lies, even as their lies change with changing circumstances. This would not be possible if they were conscious of what they are doing; by definition, it must be an unconscious process. They may, however, be aware of their shifting beliefs when they have some "down time" and are not actively engaged with others. At any rate, for some people there is a dialectic between being conscious and not conscious of their lying.

Children develop a conscience around age three to five; why some fail to do so or lose their conscience is not known with certainty. People who have lacunae in their conscience can lie and not feel any guilt or remorse. They have one of two personality disorders: narcissistic personality disorder or anti-social personality disorder. If the personality disorder is mild or moderate, these people can be treated successfully with psychoanalysis. People with severe personality disorders, however, cannot be treated with psychoanalysis. The patient's honesty is an integral part of analysis.

Lawyers, Lies, and Psychotherapists

One of my jobs is to write reports on immigrants seeking asylum in the U.S., ascertaining the validity of any psychological symptoms they report. I have found that many of these people lie in their attempt to stay in America. The most common complaint is that they suffer from Post-Traumatic Stress Disorder (PTSD) because of what they experienced at the hands of their home country's government. Much of the time, I refuse to write the report that they want me to write, so they find a psychotherapist who will.

For example, I met with a journalist from Bangladesh who said he had written stories critical of the government, and if he returned he would face harsh reprisals. During our interview, it came out that if he did get his green card, he planned to visit his family—in Bangladesh. I was supposed to believe that if he returned without receiving asylum he would be jailed or worse, but if he returned having received asylum in the U.S. he could happily visit his family. The government of Bangladesh would not care if he had received asylum in the U.S.; whether or not he returned with a green card, his fate would be the same. I refused to write the report, and he went to another psychotherapist.

The problem is widespread; an immigration lawyer once approached me to write positive reports for his clients, promising that

I could make good money doing this work. He was right; there is good money in writing positive reports. He had been working with a psychologist who churned out nothing but reports supporting the immigrants' claims, but needed to find a new psychiatrist to work with. The immigration lawyer had quite a few clients, very few of whom had legitimate claims for asylum. Many of their stories were straight-up lies. I refused his offer.

CLINICAL CASES

Summer

I have been seeing Summer for about one year. Her mother brought her to me because she was acting out. She was diagnosed with ADHD when she was eight and has been on stimulants ever since.

Summer had been seeing me for about six months when she claimed that someone had stolen her phone at gunpoint. Summer's mother was skeptical, but during our session Summer began to cry as she told the story of getting robbed. Her affect was appropriate for someone in an agitated state, and her story was internally consistent. After the session, I told her mother that I had no doubt her story was true.

A few months later, Summer's mother found the phone in Summer's room. The tears and all the rest of it had been a big lie. I was taken aback; Summer had given an Oscar-worthy performance when she lied to my face. Her mother and I thought it was true, which of course was Summer's intention. I explored about her dishonesty and the performance she gave to make it believable. She was remorseful, and I believe that she genuinely felt guilty about having lied in such a flamboyant fashion.

I believe that Summer feels remorse because her lie was for personal gain. She and her mother had been in conflict about Summer's use of social media, and her mother was threatening to take her phone away when Summer claimed she had been robbed. Since her lie was exposed, she and her mother have been getting along much better, she is no longer acting out, and her privileges have been restored.

Katy

Katy was five years old, the child of a working mother and a stay at home father. One day at school she said that her father had sexually abused her. She was sent to a psychologist and recounted—numerous times and with great consistency—exactly what her father had done to her. Katy was then examined at the ER, but no signs of sexual abuse were present. Nevertheless, the psychologist believed that Katy was telling the truth, and her father was arrested.

The District Attorney sent Katy to me for evaluation. In treatment, the following facts emerged: first, Katy had witnessed "primal scene," i.e. she saw her parents having sex. Second, her father spent a good deal of time viewing pornography, to which Katy had been exposed. In fact, what she says her father did to her is a scene from a particular pornographic movie. Finally, her father masturbated regularly, and one time some of his semen accidentally got on Katy.

My evaluation of Katy is different than the psychologist's. While I reject their conclusions, Katy's father was incredibly irresponsible and over-exposed his daughter to sexual material for which she was not developmentally ready. I do not think he had sex with Katy, but in the eyes of the court this is not a settled issue.

I was subsequently hired by the defense to testify that there had been no vaginal penetration. The father is going to spend time in jail, but how long depends (in part) on the question of whether he had sexual penetration with Katy. If I testify that there was no penetration, and the jury agrees, he will spend significantly less time in prison than he otherwise would.

Mike

Mike is in his early 60s and has been married for twenty years. He came to me and said he was addicted to prostitutes, pornography and gambling. Mike perceived his wife had no idea about the prostitutes. He said he patronized prostitutes about twice a month; Mike preferred escort services, which generally cost $300 a "visit."

Mike never uses a condom with prostitutes, though they do—except when performing oral sex. One day he told me that he had found a bump on his penis which he suspected was a genital wart. My first thought was for his wife. He had no intention of telling her, as that would reveal his secret life. Sure enough, before long, Mike's wife found a pimple in her vagina. It is quite likely a genital wart she received from her husband.

Fortunately, Mike has a conscience and feels guilty about frequenting prostitutes and (possibly) giving his wife genital warts. He feels guilty about his other addictions as well. Mike consciously does not have malicious intentions. He and his body, however, feel helpless under these strong drives and urges. We are continuing the work of understanding these urges.

COMMITMENT, LOYALTY, AND LIES

As the cases above make clear, lying comes easily even to people without serious personality disorders. This is not to minimize their guilt and remorse, but ordinary people often lie systematically. In all three cases above, one person led a secret life, a pattern of behaviors that had to be kept secret from their entire circle of family and friends. Once their secret life was established—for whatever reason—lying became necessary because to be found out would rupture these relationships, perhaps beyond repair.

The journalist Izzy Stone is credited with the truism, "governments lie." So do people who have neither narcissistic nor anti-social personality disorders. In short, ordinary people lie. Sometimes, as in the case of the people who hid Anne Frank and her family, lying is for a morally higher end. More often it is not, as with Summer, Katy's father, and Mike. In each of these cases, what perhaps began as an impulsive behavior became a pattern of behaviors—a secret life—that required systematic deception to keep surreptitious.

The degree to which these people are conscious of their lies, whether they believe them as they are telling them, is an academic concern. The practical reality is that in a marriage, especially a love marriage but also an arranged marriage, one can expect one's partner to lie. Honesty one-hundred percent of the time is an unrealistic goal. Complete honesty is certainly a laudable goal, but it is not one that can be realized by most people.

This is an object lesson that I have learned through my life experiences as well as in my psychiatric practice. I have also learned that it is far better to be with a person who has some gaps in conscience than a person who has huge lacunae in it. The former will likely betray you, but there is hope that the rupture in the relationship can be healed. But a sociopath will betray you, lie to you, and only pretend to be sorry.

CHAPTER 6
The Ubiquity of Aggression

The tendency to aggression is an innate, independent, instinctual disposition in man... it constitutes the powerful obstacle to culture.
—Sigmund Freud

Webster's English Dictionary online defines aggression as: 1) a "forceful action or procedure (as an unprovoked attack) especially when intended to dominate or master; 2) the practice of making attacks or encroachments; especially unprovoked violation by one country of the territorial integrity of another; and 3) hostile, injurious, or destructive behavior or outlook especially when caused by frustration." For psychiatric purposes, the latter definition is the most relevant.

Expanding on this definition, Auchincloss and Samberg define aggression as, "the wish to subjugate, prevail over, harm or destroy others, and the expression of any of these wishes in action, words, or fantasy" (Auchincloss and Samberg 2012, 11) This definition can be improved by emphasizing: 1) the instinctual nature of aggression; 2) the frequently unconscious nature of aggression; and 3) the behavioral aspects of aggression. Thus, I define aggression as follows: aggression is a conscious or unconscious emotional force powered by basic psychological drives that intends to harm or destroy others and/or oneself, and manifests verbally, non-verbally, and/or through action.

Aggressive impulses and drives can originate in the conscious or unconscious mind and can manifest in thought or action. In terms of psychotherapy, the more conscious a patient is of the reason for their aggression, the greater the likelihood that they will come to understand it and learn to control and/or channel it into non-destructive behaviors.

Aggression and Psychoanalysis

Most psychoanalysts have treated aggression as an object of explanation. The first, of course, was Freud, whose thinking about aggression evolved over time. In his earlier work Freud regarded aggression as derivative of libido, the unstoppable human drive towards pleasure. Freud regarded libido as the most fundamental of human drives and ultimately as the basis for all behavior. With the publication of *Beyond the Pleasure Principle*, however, Freud revised his theory by positing the existence of a second instinctual drive called Thanatos, the Greek word for death (Freud 1920). Thanatos is an instinctual drive towards death and destruction. Aggression, therefore, is not derivative of libido but is a direct manifestation of the death instinct.

Peter Gay recognizes that this was a major shift in Freud's thinking (Gay 1989). By introducing a concept antithetical to libido and its drive towards pleasure, Thanatos brought an element of internal conflict into the human psyche. Instead of the singular pursuit of pleasure, there was now an opposite drive towards destruction. Instead of one unconscious, monolithic drive motivating all human behavior, there were now two diametrically opposed drives motivating human behavior. The unconscious life of people was now a battlefield between these two opposing forces.

The magnitude of this contradiction makes pathology inevitable. In a break with his earlier work, Freud saw this pathology as not just affecting the individual but as playing out in world affairs. In *Civilization and Its Discontents*, Freud argued that organized human aggression, viz. warfare, could be attributed to Thanatos and the unconscious predilection to aggression and violence (Freud 1930). Freud's latter years were marked by pessimism regarding civilization and the progressive notion that conflict between nations could someday be eliminated.

The ego psychologists Hartman, Kris, and Lowenstein agree that aggression and libido are both innate but separate drives (Hartman, Kris, and Lowenstein 1949). Contrary to Freud, however, they contend that aggression (as a component of Thanatos) does not necessarily lead to destruction and death. Instead, they argue that aggression has a similar relation as libido to the Nirvana principle. Freud's "Nirvana principle" holds that the psyche tends towards homeostasis. Over time, libidinal drives accumulate and need to be discharged, resulting in pleasure and restoring homeostasis. If these drives are not discharged, the person will experience discomfort and, ultimately, some form of pathology.

Aggression, according to Hartman et al, works the same way as libido. Aggressive impulses build up over time, and if not discharged will lead to discomfort and pathology. Discharges of aggression need not be total; mild discharges can return the psyche to homeostasis. In accordance with Freud's pleasure principle, discharges of aggression are pleasurable and the lack of discharge is uncomfortable and will sooner or later result in pathology. Only a full discharge of aggressive drives will result in the destruction of the object (whatever or whoever this may be).

Like Freud, Winnicott considered aggression to be an instinctual "life force" and a necessary part of a person's psyche. Winnicott, however, considered aggression to be mostly a positive force, and is best known for arguing its positive virtues. For Winnicott, "there is no love without aggression, no subject, no object, no reality, and no creativity... for Winnicott, aggression is an achievement that leads to the capacity to live creatively and to experience authenticity." This stands in stark contrast to Freud's view of aggression as a manifestation of Thanatos, a drive that necessarily leads to death. For Freud, Thanatos at best results in internal conflicts of the psyche, at worst in death, destruction, and war.

CLINICAL CASES

In the course of my practice I have had the opportunity to observe and experience many cases of aggression. These experiences cover the spectrum of aggression, from aggressive talk to personal threats against me and my colleagues.

Addiction and Aggression

When I first saw Robert in a clinical setting, he was addicted to benzodiazepines and was taking Suboxone to treat his opiate addiction. He had been using for over a decade. My initial reaction was that these two substances are contra-indicated, i.e. they are a dangerous combination and Robert easily could have overdosed. Having some experience with drug users, I knew that any suggestion that he get off one or both substances would most likely be met with hostility. So I met with him a few times before broaching the subject of his drug use and the dangerous combination he was using.

After a few sessions, I suggested that we can gradually wean himself off one drug at a time. I soon realized that my previous experience with drug users was inadequate preparation for Robert's reaction. He immediately became agitated, irritable, and began arguing with me. His anger started escalating and for safety concerns, I decided to end the session. Towards the end of our session, he was so agitated that I worried for my safety. My fear was grounded in reality, as he threatened me physically as he was leaving my office.

I was able to keep him at the clinic, and with the help of clinic staff was able to calm him down. As his aggression subsided, to my surprise he expressed guilt over his behavior. He also exhibited signs of remorse and apologized for threatening me. I was pleased for him, and relieved for myself.

Research has shown that differences in neurobiology influence the type of aggression a patient presents. Robert's aggression was explosive, irrational, and emotional; it was a "hot" response (Martin and Volkmar 2007). Patients who are calculating and manipulative, whose aggression is often characterized as "cold," have different brain physiologies than patients like Robert. But Robert's drug addiction complicates the diagnostic process. Was his aggressive response caused by his brain physiology, the effects of drug abuse, or both?

This question is difficult to answer from the examination of a single patient. Robert's addiction clearly did not mitigate his aggression. But the relatively quick de-escalation of his aggression, and his remorse over threatening me, indicate that he is hard-wired for "hot" aggression. If his aggression was of the cold, calculating variety, he would have shown no remorse. Indeed, most likely he would not have reacted violently but would have tried to manipulate me into maintaining his addiction.

The issue of hot vs. cold aggression is more than an academic question; it has real legal consequences. In the U.S., a person who commits an aggressive and/or violent act that is deemed to be cold and calculating will, if convicted, face harsher punishment than a person who commits an act of aggression deemed to have been committed impulsively. Persons who commit impulsive crimes are seen as having less control over their actions and, therefore, are less responsible for their actions than the calculating criminal.

At any rate, it is safe to say that addicts are (by definition) attached to their drugs, and anyone standing between them and their substances should be prepared for an aggressive—if not violent—response.

Aggression and Self-Definition

When Milo came to see me, he was already involved in a bitter legal dispute. The following happened before Milo came to see me.

Milo was born in Greece and immigrated to the U.S. 20 years ago. He became an owner of a number of apartment buildings, and had a superintendent working for him. For reasons that were never fully clear, Milo got into a conflict with the superintendent when he refused to pay him for overtime the super had worked. Milo claimed that his super had not done a good job, so he was not going to pay him. The superintendent subsequently filed a lawsuit against Milo for his overtime pay.

Before a trial, lawyers take depositions from the plaintiff, defendant, and any and all witnesses. Milo was married to a much younger woman; he was 62 years old, she was 25. At some point during the deposition, Milo claimed the superintendent's lawyer insulted his wife by calling her a concubine. This sent Milo into a rage; he shouted at the lawyer and threatened to sue him and cause him to lose his license to practice law. (It was never clear how Milo intended to achieve the latter.) At any rate, Milo vowed to destroy the lawyer.

This is when Milo first came to see me, his young wife in tow. He did all the talking; she was very passive. Milo claimed that he and his wife had suffered emotional stress because of the lawyer's comments. He said he and his wife had problems eating, sleeping, and carrying out their daily routines and responsibilities. Then he offered to pay for ten sessions up front, though I sensed that he had no intention of attending all ten sessions. What he wanted from me was a report that said he and his wife were suffering the aforementioned emotional stress. I did not say so, but I considered his offer to pre-pay as a bribe. I refused the offer. I did not write the report that Milo wanted me to, but I did write that his wife was suffering from adjustment disorder. This was enough for the court to push back his trial date by three months. This is all I know of Milo's case because after I wrote the report I never saw him again.

Milo was not serious about getting therapy, and I remain unconvinced that he was suffering emotionally in the way he described. However, Milo clearly had anger issues.

Based on my observations of his behavior and his self-reporting, I believe Milo had a narcissistic personality structure. He was obviously proud that as a 62 year old man he could attract a 25 year old wife. This was integral to his identity, as was his ostensible economic success. When his self-conception was challenged, he flew into a rage completely disproportionate to the situation. In addition, his wife was extremely passive, hardly saying a word in any of our sessions. These are all symptoms indicative of a narcissistic personality disorder. Again, this is not a formal diagnosis, which would require many more sessions and—most importantly—that Milo be serious about his therapy.

The Stay at Home Rapist

Dorothy was a single mother with an eight year old daughter when she began dating John. After a few months, John moved in with Dorothy and her daughter. He worked sporadically, spending much of his time at home. This did not bother Dorothy; she was lonely and liked John's companionship.

John lived with Dorothy for eight years. Dorothy had a steady job and was usually not at home. But John often was, and he was often not alone. A simple Google search would have revealed (and eventually did) that John was a convicted sex offender and a pedophile. He began molesting Dorothy's daughter soon after he moved in; this continued for the eight years that he lived with them. Dorothy claims to have been oblivious to what was happening, claiming that the sexual abuse occurred when she was at work.

This may or may not be true, but when Dorothy's daughter was 16 she told a friend at school that her mother's boyfriend was molesting her. Her friend told a teacher who alerted child protective services; the ensuing investigation confirmed that John had been sexually abusing Dorothy's daughter for almost eight years. When she (claimed) to first hear of this, Dorothy did a Google search on John and found that indeed he was a convicted sex offender.

John ended up in jail, but this did not help Dorothy's daughter. She began to engage in high-risk activities of all kinds, including drug use, promiscuity, and self-harm. She got pregnant and had an abortion; when she wasn't paralyzed by depression, she was wild and out of control. Years of sexual abuse had created an enormous amount of aggression in Dorothy's daughter. But instead of channeling her anger positively, she was turning it inward and engaging in self-destructive behavior.

THE TEPID MEAN OF MARRIAGE

In *Civilization and Its Discontents* Freud argues that libido and Thanatos, the life-instinct and the death instinct, are in a constant state of conflict with each other and are fundamentally anti-social in nature (Freud 1930). Both are pure Id, and if they were not restrained by the Superego (conscience) society would be impossible. People's drive for sex and destruction would lead to a war of all against all. As individuals, the Superego keeps people's sex drive and aggressive impulses in check, which also makes possible socially normative behavior.

There is a price for civil behavior, however, and Freud paints a gloomy view of the restraint necessary for society and for effective functioning in the world. When our instincts are negative, we learn to restrain them as we mature. This restraint, in turn, leads to a sense of dissatisfaction. True satisfaction would be had if we let our sexual and aggressive instincts run wild, but this would destroy us—probably sooner rather than later. Thus, dissatisfaction is the price of civilization. Freud characterizes restraint of the instincts, what we could call good mental health, as "the tepid mean between ecstasy and depression."

The cases presented above suggest that marriage is similar to Freud's conception of society. In all three cases, one or more individuals acted aggressively and outside the norms of society. If one or both spouses in a marriage lose control of their instincts, it is unlikely that their marriage will last. While some unrestrained behavior is exciting, it is also dangerous to the marriage, especially if it is more than episodic. So, for this point of view, the successful marriage is neither exciting nor destructive, but strikes a mean between these two. Hopefully, it will be superior to "a tepid mean between ecstasy and depression."

CHAPTER 7
The Pathology of Envy

There is perhaps no phenomenon which contains so much destructive feeling as moral indignation, which permits envy to be acted out under the guise of virtue.

—Erich Fromm

T he definitions of jealousy and envy are quite similar; some would say they are synonymous. For example, the *Oxford English Dictionary* online defines jealousy as: "Feeling or showing an envious resentment of someone or their achievements, possessions, or perceived advantages." The definition of envy is quite similar: "A feeling of discontented or resentful longing aroused by someone else's possessions, qualities, or luck." Despite the strong similarity of these definitions, psychoanalysis sees them as distinct psychological phenomena.

This distinction is defined well in *Psychoanalytic Terms and Concepts* (Auchincloss and Samberg 2012). Jealousy is "a set of painful feelings and thoughts associated with the experience of the actual or imagined advantage of a rival, especially in regard to the love of an object," whereas envy is a "negative feeling that accompanies the wish to possess an attribute of another." Jealously is painful, but this feeling is not directed outside the individual. In contrast, envy begins with the feeling of jealousy but extends outward to the other, coveting what they have. Crabb's *English Synonyms* makes the distinction more dramatically: "… Jealousy fears to lose what it has; envy is pained at seeing another have that which it wants for itself.… The envious man sickens at the sight of enjoyment" (Crabb 1917). If jealousy says, "I don't have it and I wish I did," envy says, "I don't have it and I don't want anyone else to have it."

Perhaps the most famous psychoanalytic treatment of envy is Melanie Klein's *Envy and Gratitude*, where she offers a powerful indictment of envy: "Envy spoils the capacity for enjoyment [which] explains to some extent why envy is so persistent. For it is *enjoyment* and the *gratitude* to which it gives rise that mitigate destructive impulses, envy, and greed" (Klein 1975). Klein considers gratitude to be integral to mental health and morality: "There are very pertinent psychological reasons why envy ranks among the seven 'deadly sins'. I would even suggest that it is unconsciously felt to be the greatest sin of all, because it spoils and harms the good object which is the source of life."

Klein's analysis of envy begins with the infant and its relationship with its mother. Klein contends that it is normal for infants to experience envy and anxiety. The infant's desire for milk is greater than its actual needs, so it feels deprived on a regular basis; this, in turn, is the cause of the infant's anxiety. The infant's anxiety triggers the ego defense of splitting, in which the infant's image of its mother splits into two images, the "good mother" and the "bad mother." Envy is the indirect result of the infant's splitting of the mother. At some point, the "bad mother" withholds milk from the hungry infant and the infant realizes that he cannot produce milk on his own.

The origin of envy is the infant coveting the milk that the "bad mother" is withholding from it. This primitive envy resurfaces in psychoanalysis, when the patient begins to identify the analyst as the "bad mother" and becomes unconsciously envious of the analyst. This, in turn, manifests as criticism of the analyst and the rejection of the insights the analyst (the "good mother") has to offer.

Envy also may manifest in an increase in greedy and destructive behavior by the patient. Klein argues that the good feelings that result from the "good breast" mitigate against feelings of envy. The enjoyment of the "good breast," i.e. good things in life, is the source of gratitude, which in turn mitigates against destructive impulses like greed and aggression.

CLINICAL CASES

Sylvia

Sylvia was referred to me by the District Attorney's office for court mandated treatment. Sylvia was a successful physician in her 60s who had been caught shoplifting—for the second time. This was one of those ostensibly odd cases because Sylvia and her husband (a successful plastic surgeon) made far more money than the average American; they were undeniably well-to-do. Yet the times she was caught (and the many times that she was not), Sylvia stole items that usually cost no more than $50, a price she could easily afford.

When Sylvia was caught shoplifting the first time she was given one-hundred hours of community service and the charges were dropped. The second time was similar, but in addition to the community service, she was required to undergo therapy at least twice a week for six months. If she completed her community service and her therapy requirements, the charges would be dropped. The community service proved to be the easy part of her court mandated rehabilitation.

It is an understatement to say that Sylvia was not enthusiastic about undergoing therapy. In our first meeting she was rude, unpleasant, and uncooperative. Sylvia was a cardiologist and accustomed to dealing with facts and hard data, as opposed to the "soft" data that psychiatrists deal with. She made her lack of respect for my profession perfectly clear. On occasion I was insulted by patients, but Sylvia was more vociferous than most.

One of the first things I do when a patient comes for therapy is explain my policies concerning cancellations and insurance. My cancellation policy is simple: patients need to cancel twenty-four hours in advance of their appointment, or they are responsible for the entire fee. (I do make exceptions for emergencies.) I also do not accept insurance. When I told Sylvia these rules, she became enraged and launched into a tirade against the practice of psychiatry and psychiatrists. I was informed more than once how "good I had it" compared to "real" doctors. "How can you charge for missed sessions?!" she thundered. My policy of not taking insurance also infuriated her. She demanded to know, "how can your practice survive if you don't take insurance?"

Initially, I thought Sylvia's anger might be a rebellious reaction of some sort to her court mandated treatment. Another possibility was that she did not respect psychiatry as a profession. Within a few weeks, however, I concluded that Sylvia's anger had its roots in envy.

Sylvia saw me a second time before cancelling her next session at the last minute (a good deal less than twenty-four hours in advance). She called and told me her husband was sick and she wanted to stay home and look after him. I said OK, realizing that in all likelihood she was lying but thinking, "everyone gets *one* free pass." Not long after this, she cancelled for a second time (also at the last minute), leaving me a message that she was going to New Jersey to visit a friend. She did not give me 24 hours' notice nor did she provide a legitimate excuse. I charged her for that session. A short time later, she cancelled a third time (again with insufficient notice) saying that she had to visit a friend in the hospital. I charged her for this session, too. After I billed her for the second session, she called and angrily threatened to write negative evaluations of me on websites that rate doctors. Eventually she calmed down and did not follow through with her threats.

My association with Sylvia proved to be short-lived. She stopped attending sessions after only one month, having attended five sessions and missed three (two of which I charged her for). Before I could inform the court about her status of mandated treatment, I learned that she had been arrested a third time for shoplifting.

Five appointments with a patient is not sufficient to provide an informed and accurate diagnosis. I do not know why Sylvia, a wealthy doctor married to another wealthy doctor, stole items that cost less than $50. There exists a diagnosis called, "intermittent impulse control disorder," but this tells us little about the real cause of Sylvia's behavior. Her angry outbursts about psychiatry, about my policy of not taking insurance, and her passive-aggressive behavior with respect to keeping (or not keeping) appointments indicate that she was envious of psychiatrists in general and of me in particular.

Maria

I first started treating Maria when she was twenty-five. She was born in Mexico but immigrated to the U.S. when she was six. She is now a citizen and is fluent in Spanish.

Maria presented symptoms of chronic depression. She had a number of traumatic incidents and ongoing situations in her life. Her mother had been periodically hospitalized for episodes of paranoid psychosis, her father was a womanizer, and her sister would fly into rages and attack Maria. Her mother and father were not good parents and both were emotionally unavailable. Neither did anything to protect Maria from her sister's rage. Maria withdrew emotionally and (when possible) physically, reading her Bible alone.

I began analytically oriented psychotherapy with Maria, and over a period of time she began to express her envy of me. Of course, she knew nothing about me and absolutely nothing about my personal life. But she was very imaginative and developed elaborate fantasies about my life. In all of these fantasies I was accomplished and happy—and Maria was envious of this.

Not long after Maria began expressing her envy of me, she started to report that she was working harder than usual. She was in the process of applying to medical school, and would soon be taking the MCAT. She studied very hard, and did very well on the test. Also, she had always been afraid of men; her father had not been a positive role model, and her only real boyfriend had cheated on her. Then rather abruptly, she put profiles on some dating websites and started going on dates.

Maria was unconsciously competing with her fantasy version of me, and it led her to put energy and effort into her life. It has helped alleviate her depression, though she still requires treatment. If properly channeled, envy can function as a powerful motivation in a person's life.

Zoe

Zoe was sent to me by her dissertation advisor who was worried about her deep depression. Zoe was 45, married, and had two sons. She was just finishing up her dissertation for a doctorate in a STEM discipline, but fell into a depression so deep that she could barely function. Her advisor thought quite highly of her and made it possible for her to suspend work on her degree, take some time off and get better. He made the arrangements for Zoe to undergo treatment with me.

When she was ten years old, Zoe's mother hanged herself. One day Zoe walked into a room, and her mother was hanging by a rope from the ceiling. Her father had been completely devoted to Zoe's mother and was devastated by her suicide. After her mother's death, Zoe reports that her father was so completely traumatized that he became emotionally unavailable. Some years later, her brother married and left home. Zoe was close to her brother, but says she felt nothing when he moved away. Zoe's lack of feeling at her brother's departure indicate—though it is far from definitive—that Zoe had been traumatized by her mother's suicide and may have been suffering from PTSD.

I began seeing Zoe regularly and it quickly emerged that envy was a consistent theme in Zoe's emotional life. She talked about the many people she was envious of. Eventually (and perhaps inevitably) her focus turned to me. Her envy of me was explicit, and can be seen in a fantasy she had about me that emerged during treatment. Zoe said that she was jealous of me because I hadn't lost my mother, and I was married with a child. Also, I was making good money and was running a clinic on my own, in charge of staff and psychiatrists, many of whom were older and more experienced than I was. She despaired that because I was so much happier than she, I would not be able to understand her situation or the causes of her depression.

The problem with Zoe's fantasy was that it had no basis in fact. I am certainly not the boss of the clinic where I see Zoe. Analysts are careful to reveal nothing about themselves to their clients, and I am no exception; there is no way Zoe could have known any of the things she said about me. Seen against the backdrop of Zoe's ubiquitous envy, Zoe's free-associating fantasies about me were manifestations of envy. She pictured me as incredibly happy—unrealistically so—while she was in abject misery. Then she concluded that I could never understand her reality.

Asserting that she could not trust me, Zoe began to act out in a number of ways. First, she stopped taking her medications, a dangerous thing for anyone—especially someone in Zoe's condition—to do. Next she withheld payment, claiming that her health insurance company was refusing to cover her treatment. She finally paid, but again failed to pay me the following month. Then, even though she was still very depressed, she asked me to write a letter to her advisor saying that she was healthy enough to return and finish her dissertation. I discussed with her that she still needs further stabilization before resuming work. She was not happy to hear this and she became hostile and cussed me out. I found out later that she went to a family care physician and managed to get a letter from that doctor.

For Melanie Klein, Zoe is playing out the drama of her infant envy with her therapist. She is not receiving what she wants, she does not have the milk of the "good mother, so she decides that the therapist is the "bad mother" and subsequently rejects the insights that the therapist has to offer. Zoe made the conclusion of this unconscious process perfectly clear when she proclaimed that I would never be able to understand her.

CHAPTER 8
The Pleasure and Danger of Revenge

The virtuous man contents himself with dreaming that which the wicked man does in actual life.
—Sigmund Freud

Before you embark on a journey of revenge, dig two graves.
—Confucius

I n formulating his theory of the psyche and its unconscious processes, Freud drew heavily on Greek mythology. Patricide, infanticide, incest, murderous sibling rivalry—the list goes on. There is, however, one prominent theme in Greek mythology that Freud merely touched on and which contemporary psychoanalysis has largely ignored, viz. revenge (Rosen 2007:597; Beattie 2005:513).

Greek mythology is as replete with stories of revenge as it is with the aforementioned themes. It is, therefore, surprising that revenge has received so little attention considering its importance in people's psychological constitution and behavior.

The *Oxford English Dictionary* online defines revenge as, "The action of hurting or harming someone in return for an injury or wrong suffered at their hands." This definition is a sound starting point, but for the purposes of psychoanalytic theory it lacks a number of crucial elements. First, the "injury or wrong" may be real or it may be imagined. The psychiatric literature is replete with case studies of individuals bent on revenge for wrongs they did not actually suffer but are convinced they did. Second, the dictionary definition connotes that the wronged individual is conscious of his desire for revenge. This overlooks the possible unconscious element in fantasies and acts of revenge. For example, a person may experience a slight from a lover or close friend and consciously dismiss it as inconsequential, while unconsciously he is seething with anger, hatred, and a desire to avenge the insult.

In short, the dictionary definition implies a conscious and rational relationship between the "injury or wrong" suffered by the aggrieved person when in fact his motivations and emotions may not be fully conscious or rational.

The Roots of Revenge

The ubiquity of revenge fantasies and acts of revenge indicates its importance as part of the psyche. It is usually destructive in its consequences, but so are envy, lying, hate, and other negative emotions.

What are the fundamental psychological dynamics of revenge? Ostensibly it is the wish to inflict upon the offending party a pain similar to that experienced by the person who has been wronged. Speaking charitably, it is a desire to see justice done. Less charitably, it is a desire for vengeance. The former implies that the act of revenge will be proportional to the original offense; the latter implies that the response will not be proportional and will cause greater pain for the offender than was suffered by the victim. If taken to its logical extreme the result will be the destruction of the offender.

Why people feel the need to avenge real or imagined slights, viz. the underlying reason people desire revenge, is not well understood. What is understood is the universality of this desire when one has been wronged. When people believe a person or group is responsible for pain they have suffered, they desire to return the favor and inflict pain upon that individual or group. This response appears to be "hard-wired" into the human psyche. The universality of the desire for revenge, the strong emotions that are experienced immediately after the offense, and the difficulty that most people have in letting go of their desire for revenge are evidence (albeit indirect) of the hard-wired nature of revenge.

Some evidence indicates that revenge is an evolutionary adaptation of some kind. During her observations of chimpanzees in Tanzania, the British anthropologist Jane Goodall witnessed a murderous example of primitive revenge by her primate subjects. Rosen relates Goodall's observations:

> "For reasons as yet undetermined, in 1970 our main study community began to divide. Seven males and three females with off-spring established themselves in [a different part] of the home range. By 1972 they had become a completely separate community" (Goodall 1979:606). At first, the home group chimps engaged in "displays" apparently designed to intimidate the emigres into returning home. None did, and beginning in 1974, a series of marauding "raids" consisting of lethal beatings, bitings, hitting, and kicking, usually carried out in "gang" fashion with four or five strong young chimps separating the

victims from the group and... murdering them. By 1977, all males of the... community had been killed by their former community mates (Rosen 2007:610).

Computer modelling subsequently conducted at UCLA estimated the "evolutionary survival value of group punishment of deviant behavior," suggesting the adaptive value of a primitive form of revenge (Rosen 2007:610).

A review of evidence that revenge is the product of evolution is beyond the scope of this work. Goodall's observations, however, indicate that the necessities of evolutionary adaptation hard-wired into human beings the propensity for revenge.

Psychic Characteristics of Revenge

From a psychoanalytic viewpoint, revenge provides a number of important psychic functions. To say that these functions are important is not to say that they are good for the mental health of the individual. They are not. They are, however, the psyche's response to the real or perceived harm done to the individual. In the absence of psychoanalytic understanding and treatment, they are the mind's natural reactions to the various stimuli that turn on the psychic process of revenge.

The following four points are taken from a longer list created by Rosen (2007:603-9).

First, revenge acts as a psychological defense against feeling a variety of emotions, including shame, loss, guilt, powerlessness, and mourning. Feeling and working through these emotions is difficult and uncomfortable; it is much easier to allow them to be drowned out by the "blaring fanfare" of revenge (Rosen, 2007:603). This has particularly negative effects with respect to mourning: "[by] directing rage outward, the avenger averts his psychic gaze from issues of loss and thus delays, often for years and sometimes permanently, the work of mourning" (Rosen, 2007:603).

Second, revenge creates a primitive defense characterized by a polarized view of the person. This may be accompanied by feelings of envy, sadism, greed, and Schadenfreude. In the words of Rosen, "the greater the idealization, the greater the envy, and the greater the envy, the stronger the revenge wish... To succumb to revenge enactments is to increase our regressive resort to that triad of primitive defenses—denial, projective identification, and splitting" (Rosen 2007:604).

Third, revenge can function as a way to restore one's self-esteem in the face of the harm done to one's ego. "Revenge, fueled by narcissistic rage, is an attempt to restore the grandiose self...Feeling helpless, the victim seeks control; feeling shamed and vulnerable, he creates omnipotence... his revenge becomes a primitive attempt to restore the self by giving form, structure, aim, and direction to his inchoate fury" (Rosen 2007:605).

Finally, revenge causes the ego to defend itself by resorting to sadism, though this process is not well understood. On this point, Rosen quotes Freud: "[N]o satisfactory explanation of this perversion [sadism] has been put forward and... it seems possible that a number of mental impulses are combined in it" (Rosen 2007:609).

The Target of Revenge

People who have been hurt (or imagine that they have been hurt) by another are actively fantasizing about taking vengeance on that person. If their fantasies of revenge turn into actual revenge, they may take vengeance on the person who actually harmed them. That, however, is just one possibility. A second possibility is that their vengeance will be unconsciously displaced onto a person who unconsciously reminds them of the perpetrator. This person is likely to be weaker than the actual perpetrator but resembles him in some way. A third possibility is that their vengeance takes the form of inchoate rage and they lash out at innocent people. The non-ideologically motivated mass shooter exemplifies this phenomenon. People are randomly chosen as targets, often as a matter of convenience. Finally, the rage of vengeance can be turned inward as the victim engages in various self-destructive behaviors like self-mutilation or drug abuse.

The Benefits of Sublimated Revenge

1. To the extent that revenge is fueled by anger and rage, it is possible to use the energy of these emotions for positive ends. This is most likely to happen unconsciously, though in some cases it will be done consciously. According to the psychoanalyst Warren Poland, "revenge may have... adaptive and sublimatory aspects, in the turning of passivity to activity... and the mastery of immediate rage in the service of larger aims (such as the pursuit of social justice" (Beattie 2005:513). Modern history is replete with examples of social movement leaders turning their desire for vengeance into an active pursuit of social justice.

Mohandas Gandhi, the practical and spiritual leader of India's resistance to British colonial rule is an example of the non-violent variety. Ho Chi Minh, who had been tortured by the French (along with many other future leaders of the Vietnamese revolution) is an example of the more common armed resistance to colonial rule. He could have easily let his rage devolve into bitterness, passivity, or inchoate violence. Instead, he led a long, bloody, and ultimately successful fight against imperialism (though he did not live to see it succeed).

Most people who successfully sublimate vengeful rage are not famous revolutionaries. This does not, however, diminish sublimation's potential for positive change, whether personal, political, or both.

The Fox, the Farmer, and Mutually Assured Destruction

One of Aesop's fables is about a fox who wandered into a farmer's field containing large, juicy pumpkins. He saw no one around so he quickly bit into a big, delicious pumpkin. Just as he finished eating it, the farmer who owned the field ran up to him and said, "How dare you eat my pumpkin!"

"Please sir," said the fox, "I was hungry and I ate just one of them." But the angry farmer took a piece of cloth and dipped it in kerosene oil. Then he tied the flammable cloth around the fox's tail and set it on fire. Suddenly the fox's tail was ablaze and he was in great pain. Now the fox was furious. "You are punishing me for just one pumpkin. Now I will take my revenge!"

The fox ran into the farmer's field where ripe wheat was waiting to be harvested. The fox jumped around the field with his tail burning, igniting the crops and destroying them entirely. As he incinerated the farmer's crops, the fire spread to the rest of his body and the fox died.

The farmer thought, "If I had forgiven the fox for eating one pumpkin, he would not have burned my entire crop. Now I am ruined."

This fable points out that the pursuit of revenge often leads to mutual destruction. The fox died and the farmer was ruined. (There was no opportunity for the fox to "serve his revenge cold.") Earlier I argued that revenge can be a positive force, but this is the exception. The desire for revenge is almost always a negative force, and acting on this desire more often than not brings mutual ruin. I do not intend this as an ethical principle or moral lesson, but as an observation of reality.

There are, of course, exceptions. Just as some criminals get away with their crimes, some who pursue revenge succeed in harming or destroying the person who has wronged them without getting hurt themselves. Their revenge is successful and they get away with it. Those who are willing to take this risk are likely to take sadistic satisfaction in hurting the other person and in getting away with it. These people are quite likely anti-social personalities and lack a conscience and any sense of remorse. They are sociopaths.

To be clear, I am speculating, making educated guesses about such individuals. Sociopaths are notoriously immune to any sort of psychotherapy, and a self-satisfied sociopath is unlikely to seek psychotherapy. Thus, speculation and educated guesses are all that anyone can offer. But getting away with revenge is akin to getting away with murder in that most people do not. Morality aside, the best course for anyone seriously contemplating revenge, unless they are willing to sacrifice their own life in so doing, is to somehow work through the emotions associated with revenge, ideally letting them go. Otherwise, be sure to dig two graves.

CLINICAL CASES

Graveyard Fantasies

Early in my career I worked in the psychiatric ER of a local hospital. It was common for people—mostly women—to overdose on various medications and be rushed to the hospital. All suicide attempts are to be taken seriously, but none of the patients I treated died or seriously hurt themselves. During interviews with these patients they usually admitted that their motivation for attempting suicide was to "get even" with their boyfriend, girlfriend, or spouse. These patients were angry, hurt, and impulsively acting out. When they overdosed, many were fantasizing about making their partners feel guilty, hoping their partners would feel responsible for causing their death. Many of these patients reported having a mental image of their ex standing over their grave or at their funeral, inconsolable at having caused their lover's suicide.

My colleagues and I interpreted these suicide attempts as revenge for some real or imagined offense. At the risk of sounding glib, Confucius' maxim applies to those patients who succeed in killing themselves.

Revenge and Social Media

Even though revenge and the emotions that fuel it can be harnessed for positive ends, usually they are not. Those who go beyond revenge fantasies and act on their vengeance successfully, harming or destroying the object of their rage are just as likely to harm or destroy themselves. Confucius advised that those seeking revenge "dig two graves." Confucius was merely offering practical advice based on his observations of how revenge usually plays out. In a more Machiavellian vein, someone (nobody is certain who) once said that revenge is a dish best served cold. In other words, if you are planning to rain vengeance upon your enemies, it is best to wait until they have forgotten that they wronged you. This is also less a profound philosophical statement than practical (if morally questionable) advice.

The first case illustrates well the "two graves" principle. Early in my practice I treated the wife of an accomplished surgeon with an excellent reputation who held a prestigious position in a renowned hospital. Both he and his wife were Egyptian immigrants who had been in this country for decades.

One night they argued, and she claimed he pushed her. He did not hit her, but she called the police anyway. It is neither clear nor important what the argument was about. What is important is the vengeful actions of the wife after the police arrived. The doctor was handcuffed and taken to jail, but the wife did not press charges and he was released later that night. What she did do was covertly take pictures of her husband in handcuffs and post them on social media. If she had not done this, his employer might never have learned of the incident; even if they had it is likely that nothing would have come of it. But when the hospital saw the pictures on social media, the surgeon was promptly fired.

The irony of this incident is that the wife hurt herself as much as she hurt her husband, if not more. Because of his reputation, he quickly found another job. Their marriage, however, was seriously damaged, perhaps beyond repair. The wife did have trauma in her past, having witnessed her father get stabbed while haggling in a public market. She never processed this trauma, but how much a role it played in her vindictive behavior is an open question. It certainly does not excuse her behavior.

TWO GRAVES

For our purposes, the moral of this story is that the successful pursuit of revenge by one spouse against the other will damage if not destroy the marriage. The impulse for revenge comes from the id, the bundle of aggressive and sexual forces that must be contained if the individual—and, indeed, society—is to survive. Clearly, the impulse for revenge must be contained if a marriage is to survive.

CHAPTER 9

Hate

If you hate a person, you hate something in him that is part of yourself. What isn't part of ourselves doesn't disturb us.

—Herman Hesse

The dissolution of a marriage is frequently accompanied by one or both parties declaring their hatred for the other person. It is surprising, then, that so little has been written about hate from a psychoanalytic perspective. The psychoanalytic literature contains few discussions of hate; before the 1970s, only six psychoanalysts had written about it as a phenomenon in itself (Downey 2004).

The *Merriam-Webster Dictionary* online defines hate as: 1) an intense hostility and aversion usually deriving from fear, anger, or sense of injury; and 2) extreme dislike or antipathy. A more psychoanalytic definition focuses on the frustration of desires: "Hate defines a state of enmity toward an object that in one way or another has frustrated pleasure or desire, that is, an object in reality or fantasy is construed as having contributed to the hater's unpleasure" (Downey 2004). Others emphasize the psychological grip hatred can have on a person: "Hate means holding on to an internal object in an unforgiving way with an unyielding wish for vengeance and the destruction of the object" (Gabbard and Winer 1994).

From these and other influences I have developed my own definition of hate. *Hate is a set of mixed emotions which includes aggression and envy, in conscious or unconscious form, manifested in fantasy or action with multiple aims, one of which is to destroy.* My definition encompasses the emotional roots and ultimate aims of hate, as well as the fact that it can be conscious or unconscious. The latter adds an additional dimension to the definition of hatred, one that is found empirically when people hate themselves and/or others without being conscious that one is doing so.

Functions and Causes

There is some agreement in the literature that hate is related to the organization of the ego and can perform important psychic functions. Gabbard and Winer argue that "the functions of hate include organizing the ego, providing a sense of continuity from day to day, and fending off psychotic disorganization. Hateful transferences may conceal longings for love and acceptance" (Gabbard and Winer 1994). This view also points to the role hate can play in organizing ego functions and how it can unconsciously mask feelings of love through reaction formation. Indeed, hate is a part of life and— consciously or unconsciously—"it is mixed and intermingled with love" (Downey 2004).

What causes people to feel hatred? Are we born hard-wired to hate, do we learn it, or is it some combination of the two? In his discussion of Freud and Horney's work on hate, Gershman summarizes Horney's view:

> [Horney] maintains that the psychological structure which we call personality is the culmination of the innumerable contacts and interpersonal relationships that the child has in its course of development. The child has an innate capacity to develop a mature character and personality, provided his development is not marred by pathological interpersonal relationships, such as discrimination, injury, emotional deprivation, hate (Gershman 1947).

Horney views hate as a product of one's environment, especially if it contains pathological elements. This contrasts with Freud's view that hate is a singular manifestation of Thanatos, the death instinct, which in his later years he viewed as being a drive equal to libido in its power and effects. Freud saw Thanatos and libido as instinctual drives, whereas Horney sees hate as a product of childhood development within a particular environment.

Galdston agrees with those who say that hatred can help the ego function properly, considering hate to be "a mode of relating to objects that rests upon, and contributes to, the attainment of object constancy, a psychic achievement needed for effective ego functioning" (Galdston 1987:371). Gladston constructs a "clinical typology" of people "with regard to their competence to hate–those who are unable to hate, those who cannot stop hating, and those who have learned both how to hate and how to get over hating." Those in the first group are meek, directionless "losers" who are unable to achieve their goals; "their ship never comes in." People who cannot stop hating are either conscious or unconscious of their hate; the latter sub-group suffers from greater psychopathology, including marital problems. The third group—those who know how to hate and how to get over it—have the greatest potential for success individually and in relationships. They can choose to let go of their hate and move on with their lives. The ability to get over and learn from their hate is the "hallmark of the ego's capacity to adapt aggression in the service of desire with respect for reality" (Galdston 1987:373).

There is one psychoanalyst, however, who views hate as *sometimes* acting as a positive force. It is, at least, the most positive force available to the individual who employs it. Hate can function as a form of sustaining object relations. If individuals ascertain that they may be forgotten, that they may become an object of apathy, they will hate and/or make themselves hate able in order to maintain their attachment to the object. Bollas calls this "loving hate" and argues that although it is pathological, it is less likely to result in serious pathology than if the person cannot maintain a meaningful relationship to the object. Love is sublimated into hate which—unlike apathy—maintains a connection to the object. This is especially true in childhood development, when the establishment of stable object relations is of primary importance (Bollas 1984).

Unlike the hate hypothesized by Freud, "loving hate" is not necessarily destructive in intent. Its primary intent is to bind one to the other.

Such hate is fundamentally nondestructive in intent, and, although it may have destructive consequences—in a larger sense it can be considered destructive—the aim of such hate may be to act out an unconscious form of love. I am inclined to term this "loving hate," by which I mean a situation where an individual preserves a relationship by sustaining a passionate negative cathexis of it. If the person cannot do so by hating the object he may accomplish this passionate cathexis by being hateable and inspiring the other to hate him... Viewed this way, hate is not the opposite of love, but a substitute. A person who hates with loving passion does not dread retaliation by the object; on the contrary, he welcomes it. What he does live in fear of is *indifference*, of not being noticed or seen by the other (Bollas 1984:222).

Love is always the first choice, but when confronted with indifference hate can be a usable fallback. From this perspective, hate is preferable to apathy, the true opposite of love and hate.

Most psychoanalysts view hate as having a two-fold quality: on one hand, the development of hate is a necessary part of psychological development. In this sense, it is similar to the capacity to lie. On the other hand, under certain conditions hate can be a destructive force if it develops into psychopathology:

It is in hate's pathological forms where it is increasingly abstracted and divorced from any connection with love that it becomes noxious, contaminating, and destructive to human relationships... It seems to me that it is as development proceeds that frustration, infantile omnipotence, and defensive measures against passivity and helplessness, turn part of the aggressive energies into hostility and hatred and ultimately, if the conditions of frustration and neglect are right, into Psychopathology (Downey 2004).

External obstacles, neglect, abuse and similar factors can create psychopathology that is built on a foundation of hatred.

One manifestation of hatred that is always associated with pathology is self-hatred. According to Horney, people develop unrealistic "idealized images" of themselves based on who they would ideally like to be. Moments of realistic self-appraisal result in either feelings of "neurotic pride" or self-hatred. If the self-appraisal seems to align with the idealized self, the person will feel neurotic pride, a "temporary good feeling." If a person falls short in his self-appraisal, the result is self-hatred:

> Self-hatred is incurred whenever the "real me" does not live up to the standards, aims, demands, or claims of the idealized image. Since the latter is quite removed from reality, by contrast the real me with its realistic attributes and achievement is shrunken, insignificant, small, hateful, and contemptible. This feeling, of course, saps real self-confidence and failure ensues. The failure is then accepted as ultimate proof of the correctness of the accusation of the idealized self. Profound depression or lesser degrees of self-hatred may follow (Gershman 1947:55).

No person ever engages in a completely realistic self-appraisal; the latter is tainted by innumerable internal and external factors. Thus a feedback loop can occur where depression and self-hatred deepen as the individual's self-appraisals are increasingly affected by their depression and self-hatred.

CLINICAL CASES

Claire

Hatred often takes the form of self-hate, and early in my practice I treated "Claire," a 17-year old whose mother was Hispanic and father African-American. She presented depression and anxiety, and I treated her with medication management and analytically oriented psychotherapy. I prescribed Zoloft for Claire's depression and clonazepam for her anxiety. Her mother always accompanied Claire to her sessions.

Claire suffered from extremely low self-esteem and chronically engaged in self-harming behavior. She would often say that she hated herself, in particular her appearance. Claire had darker skin than her mother, but much lighter than her father. Her hair was curly and resembled that of most African-Americans. Claire grew up in a predominantly white neighborhood, and kids would tease her about her dark skin and the consistency of her hair. She frequently expressed the wish that her skin was lighter—like her mother's—and that her hair was more "white." Her complaints conveyed a great deal of bitterness about her appearance which manifested itself in self-destructive behaviors.

The self-destructive behaviors that Claire engaged in were similar to "cutting" behavior. Most of the time she took her medications as prescribed, but there was an instance when she tried to overdose on clonazepam. She only took a few pills, so Claire did not require a trip to the hospital. I did not regard it as a serious attempt at suicide, but any behavior of this type by a patient is not to be taken lightly. Claire would also take showers with water so hot it would burn her skin; she also burned herself with candle wax.

Dissatisfaction with her appearance was not the only factor in Claire's self-hatred. After a few months of therapy, Claire divulged that she had been sexually abused by her grandmother's boyfriend. When Claire was nine years old, she went into her grandmother's bedroom and the boyfriend was alone in the room. He molested her and the molestation continued until Claire was twelve. Instead of directing anger or hatred at the perpetrator, Claire felt that it was her fault that she was sexually assaulted, and she felt guilty about it. She would say, "If only I hadn't gone into the bedroom that day, it never would have happened. It's my fault." Claire's self-hatred manifested in self-harm and feelings of guilt about something that was definitely not her fault.

Claire eventually went to college, in a different state, and I arranged for her to see a new psychiatrist.

Claire's case is paradigmatic of self-hatred acted out in behavior. Claire thought that her actions led to her being sexually abused; she blamed herself for the sexual abuse she endured, which led to her self-destructive behavior.

Kate

Kate was from London, England, the daughter of well-to-do professionals. She was 21 when she came to New York City to attend art school. She presented with bipolar symptoms, and I prescribed Lamictal, a mood stabilizer. Her subsequent behavior evoked in me a strong countertransference.

Kate engaged in reckless sexual behavior; she had many partners and usually had unprotected sex. For a time she was seeing a man in his 40s who used drugs, would dress up as a woman and prostitute himself to other men. He would then have unprotected sex with Kate, refusing to use condoms. Kate used oral contraceptives, which interact with Lamictal, requiring me to adjust the dose. Oral contraceptives prevent pregnancy, but they do not prevent the transmission of STDs.

Kate was engaging in high-risk sexual behaviors as soon as she arrived in New York. After a few months, she began acting inappropriately vis-à-vis my relationship with her. It started with emails to me that she would send late at night saying that she was suicidal. I directed her to seek emergency services.

Then Kate began cancelling appointments at the last minute. Her excuse the first time was that she had forgotten about a test she had the next day for which she needed to study. I did not believe her, but I did not charge her; it was her first cancellation, she met the criteria for high risk, and I felt I should see her at least once a month so I could be sure that there was no interaction between her mood stabilizer and the oral contraceptives. Also, after cancelling she asked me to send a refill for her

Lamictal. This made me uncomfortable because she was high risk and needed close monitoring.

The next month she called a few hours before her appointment to say that she was flying to London to visit her family and again requested a refill of Lamictal. I expressed my displeasure and told her this was concerning to me, given the fact that I hadn't seen her for almost three months and she was a patient who needed close monitoring. Of course, it happened a third time and I had to put my foot down; I referred her to a different practitioner closer to where she was living and where there was a medical center well-equipped to provide psychiatric services for high risk patients.

Kate's response was to write a scathing review of me online, full of exaggeration and outright lies. When we parted ways, Kate ostensibly hated me—at least if her review is any indication. Likewise, Kate brought up strong counter-transference in me; I found myself not liking her and wanting to get rid of her as a patient, though I used my countertransference productively to help her. Kate had borderline personality organization which was evident in her fragmented identify and predominantly splitting based defenses.

Wendy

Wendy was a middle-aged woman referred to me by a psychologist for medication management. I only saw her three times; I include her because of the intense feelings she brought up in me. When she first came to my office and saw that I was from India, she asked me if I had gone to medical school in the United States or in India. "India," I replied. I could tell that she immediately held this against me. This was confirmed when she went back to the referring psychologist and complained about my training, assuming that it was inferior to medical school in the U.S. He was able to convince her that my credentials were sound, and I did my residency, fellowship and advanced training in the U.S. She agreed to come back.

She was not the only one who needed convincing to come back. I was hesitant to be her psychiatrist, given her skepticism regarding my credentials and ability. But the referring psychologist talked me into at least doing an intake evaluation, after which I could decide whether to continue with her or not.

I found Wendy to be an incredibly hateful and unpleasant person. The majority of the intake session revolved around how she hated everything, including her psychiatrist, her husband, and her job.

The evaluation session was more dramatic than I had anticipated. Wendy came with her husband, who during the session said that he intended to divorce her. Wendy was hearing this for the first time, and burst into tears. I did my best to calm her down.

She began to make remarks like, "how long does one go to medical school in India," "how effective is the training there," and that I looked too young and inexperienced to be a good psychiatrist. I was not alone in this, as she hated her previous psychiatrist and wanted to switch. By the end of the session, she expressed how she hates doctors who went to medical school outside the United States and thinks they are unfit to treat her. I felt relieved that she would not be my patient and wished her well.

CHAPTER 10
Evil

Humanity has wrestled with the nature and causes of evil since we developed brains capable of abstract thought. Although usually the purview of theologians and philosophers, few psychoanalysts have provided insights into the nature of evil and why people commit evil acts. Their views of evil and its relation to the human person constitute a broad spectrum of opinion, from those who think we should speak only of evil acts to those who think that some people are inherently evil.

The first point on the spectrum of psychoanalytic opinion is the idea that we should speak only of evil acts, not evil people. Horne argues that to speak of "evil people" prevents one from explaining their evil behavior (Horne 2008). By defining some people as evil, the question of why these people commit evil acts is answered before it can be asked. In other words, by labelling someone as evil, we think that we have explained their behavior when all we have done is give them a totalizing label that mitigates against an actual explanation. Horne advocates using the term evil as an adjective and not as a noun:

> [Evil] should be employed to qualify acts of persons rather than their character. This change would enable us to eschew foundational explanations of evil and, therefore, to examine evil acts in their contexts and so better discern their nature and motivation (Horne 2008:669).

Horne does not feel that people are intrinsically evil. Rather, "evil is an adjective that refers to the characteristics of particular acts and not to the character of the perpetrators of those acts" (Horne 2008:675). Only when the locus of evil is the evil action—not the person who commits those acts—is an explanation of those acts possible.

The middle ground in this debate is staked out by Hering, who argues that while "evil" should not be rejected entirely, we should "try to find another word which has less moralistic, judgmental and hypocritical undertones." Hering believes that all of us have the potential for committing evil acts, and that we unconsciously recoil from this perception by labelling those who do commit evil acts with the all-encompassing label "evil."

> [I]n this way the notion of 'evil' not only serves to name a real threat but also to distance us from the disturbing insight of how much more we ordinary human beings might have in common with the designated perpetrator of [evil acts].

By not labelling people as inherently evil, we can more accurately assess "what constitutes a threat of 'evil' from outside" while remembering our own potential for evil. In so doing, we avoid dehumanizing the perpetrators of evil behavior (Hering 1997:209-217).

The other end of the spectrum is well-represented by Michael H. Stone in his *The Anatomy of Evil* (Stone 2010). Stone was influenced by his work at the New York State Psychiatric Institute, where he treated (to the extent possible) some of the worst people humanity has to offer. As the reviewer Richard C. Friedman writes, "As a group they are more depraved than anyone that this reviewer has met in the world of fiction. Most have been more vicious than Goneril, Regan, Edmund, Richard the III, and Hannibal Lecter of best seller and film fame. These are not people that most psychotherapists ever meet, unless they happen to be murdered by one of them" (Friedman 2010: 361). Stone's experience with people who have committed unspeakable acts led him to the conclusion that some people are intrinsically evil and are immune to the techniques of psychoanalysis. There is nothing that can remove from them whatever it is that makes them evil; they are irredeemable.

To illustrate his theory, Stone constructs a 22-point "gradations of evil" scale, from least evil to most evil. The first entry is people who have killed in self-defense and have no traces of psychosis. They are not evil people. Stone's scale, however, quickly moves into the realm of those who are intrinsically evil. The 22nd entry is psychopathic torturer-murderers for whom torture is the primary motive. Fortunately, most people do not fit anywhere on this scale. Stone thinks that *some* people are intrinsically evil, not *all* people.

Unlike most other psychoanalysts writing about evil, Stone defines what constitutes evil behavior. Acts that society deems evil have the following characteristics:

- The act must be breathtakingly horrible
- Malice aforethought usually precedes the act (i.e., it is done in cold blood)

- The degree of suffering inflicted will be wildly excessive
- The nature of the act will appear wildly incomprehensible, bewildering, and beyond the imagination of ordinary people in the community

Psychoanalytic treatments of evil acts focus on the individual pathology that causes a person to behave in ways that normal society deems evil. There are periods in history, however, when entire nations seem to have collectively lost their moral compass and engage in evil on a national scale. In these historical instances, "ordinary people in the community" are either actively engaged in heinous acts or are complicit in them by virtue of their acquiescence. One of the most notorious instances of this—and likely the best known to the contemporary reader—is the Holocaust, the systematic extermination of 6 million Jews and 5 million others in Nazi Germany.

The Holocaust did not happen because 60 million Germans suddenly became psychotic killers. Large scale slaughters of this kind do not require mass psychosis (if such a thing exists). In *Eichmann in Jerusalem: A Report on the Banality of Evil*, Hannah Arendt argues that not even the small percent of the German population who carried out the atrocities of the Holocaust were psychotic (Arendt 1964). Arendt covered the trial of Adolf Eichmann for the *New Yorker* after the Mossad captured him in Argentina and brought him to Israel to stand trial in 1960. Eichmann was a member of the elite Nazi SS and was the third highest ranking official in that organization.

What struck Arendt as she watched Eichmann's trial was the absolute ordinariness of Eichmann. He struck Arendt as a person of average intelligence who in most contexts would be considered sane, albeit boring. He held racist and anti-Semitic views—common among Germans at the time—but was otherwise conventional in temperament and tastes. Yet this man was responsible for organizing much of the logistics of the Holocaust, including coordinating the railway routes that would carry eleven million people to their deaths.

Arendt's point is simple: ordinary people who are not mentally ill can be complicit in mass murder. The population of an entire country can be complicit in genocide, as was the case in Nazi Germany (with some notable and heroic exceptions). Adolf Eichmann was evil without fitting into Michael Stone's 22 "gradations of evil" scale. His evil was not a product of psychopathology, but of the place he occupied in a bureaucracy dedicated to the systematic extermination of millions of people. Like most of the Nazis who were captured and put on trial, his defense was that he was "just following orders." And indeed he was. The orders, as part of the Final Solution and the political system from whence they came were the locus of evil.

The phenomenon of ordinary people committing heinous acts is complex and beyond the scope of this work. I touched on it merely to point out that the evil seen in our world is not merely the work of psychopathic murderers; indeed, a solid argument can be made that the majority of evil acts are committed by ordinary people who, like Eichmann, believe that they are doing the right thing.

CLINICAL CASES

Natasha

Natasha was of Middle Eastern origin and worked as a flight attendant for an international airline. She was referred to me by a colleague to evaluate her suitability for analysis. She was young and attractive, but complained of not being able to find a man who she liked sufficiently to have a relationship with. She also complained of anger issues.

Natasha had lacunae in her superego functioning, i.e. she had questionable moral principles. First she told me a story about a passenger on a flight who kept ringing the help bell. On the third ring he requested a Coke. Natasha was annoyed and angered by this, and spit in his drink. I was taken aback that she could be so petty and easily angered. Then she told me about her 92-year-old mother who was suffering from dementia. Her mother has a bell to summon help from Natasha or other caregivers. One day she was—in Natasha's estimation—ringing the bell too frequently. Natasha proceeded to slap her. Again I was stunned by this statement, but I tried to determine if Natasha felt any remorse for these behaviors.

She did not. After some probing questions, Natasha stated flatly that she was engaging in "tit for tat" behavior, that this is the way the world works, and that she did not feel guilty for what she had done.

Natasha engaged in evil acts, but was probably not an intrinsically evil person like those that Michael Stone observed. I have, however, come into contact with such people.

Mother's Last Ride

I was called by the District Attorney to be an expert witness for a particularly grisly murder. One day a young man who was a paranoid schizophrenic took an Uber ride carrying a plastic garbage bag that emitted a terrible smell, prompting the driver to call the police. It turns out that the bag contained parts of the young man's mother, whom he had murdered and chopped into pieces. Before calling Uber, he took a selfie of himself and the bag containing what had been his mother, smiling ear-to-ear. The actions of this young man can safely be called evil.

The defense wanted me to testify that he was not guilty by reason of insanity. While clearly insane, I had qualms about testifying to his insanity. Part of me felt that he deserved prison, even though being committed for life to a state psychiatric hospital is not much better. I was experiencing an internal moral conflict, so I declined to take the case.

Whatever became of that young man, he almost certainly fell into Stone's category of inherently evil people who are difficult to be treated with psychoanalysis. For me and most of society, the most important resolution of this case was that he was separated from society for the rest of his life.

Bloody Pajamas

I was working in the ER when the paramedics brought an eight-year-old girl to the hospital. She was in her pajamas, which were covered in blood. I was told that her father had just stabbed her mother to death, apparently in a jealous rage over the wife's real or imagined infidelity. I was shocked; my own child was about her age. I composed myself, only to wonder what my role was in this situation. What could I possibly do for this girl? What could I possibly say to her? What could anyone possibly say?

Eventually she was admitted to the child inpatient unit. I would go check up on her during visitation hours, and saw that she noticed the other children's parents bringing food and treats for them. The girl asked me repeatedly when her mother was going to bring her something. Children her age understand the concepts relative to her situation; perhaps she was in denial from the trauma of her experience. At any rate, I was once again at a loss for anything meaningful to say; I simply did my best to comfort her. Her mother was dead, her father would be in prison for life or at least for a very long time, and she was bound for the Russian roulette that is the foster care system. (Some foster parents are better than others.)

I present this case for two reasons: first, to show that evil acts affect others, especially the most vulnerable among us. This point is obvious but too often gets lost in the sensational nature of crimes like these. When people hear of horrible murders and other evil actions, the common response is shock and horror at the act. Those left in the aftermath often do not get the attention they deserve. Secondly, I wanted to highlight that all the helping professions, psychiatry included, have their limits. When horrible things happen to innocent people, often the most compassionate and experienced professionals are not in a position to do or say anything meaningful. Even if one could explain why the husband murdered his wife, what good would it do this little girl? If certain conditions are met, understanding can facilitate healing; unfortunately, this is not always the case.

CHAPTER 11
Empathy: Walking in Another's Shoes

The *Oxford English Dictionary* online defines sympathy as, "Feelings of pity and sorrow for someone else's misfortune," while empathy is defined as, "The ability to understand and share the feelings of another." Confusion between empathy and sympathy is common. Unlike sympathy, empathy involves trying to understand how another person is feeling and thinking. Sympathy is the feeling evoked by the difficulties experienced by another person; empathy involves trying to understand what and how another person is thinking and feeling.

Psychiatrists and psychoanalysts try to empathize with their patients while also sympathizing with them. Webster's Dictionary offers a definition that better reflects this goal: empathy is, "the action of understanding, being aware of, being sensitive to, and vicariously experiencing the feelings, thoughts, and experience of another of either the past or present without having the feelings, thoughts, and experience fully communicated in an objectively explicit manner." This is quite similar to the definition given by Auchincloss and Samberg: empathy is a "complex affective and cognitive process of feeling, imagining, thinking, and somatically sensing one's way into the experience of another person" (Auchincloss and Samberg 2012).

Empathy does not necessarily involve feelings of sympathy for the other person. One can feel empathy without feeling sympathy. Military thinkers from Clausewitz (*On War*) to Sun Tzu (*The Art of War*) have recognized the importance of understanding how the enemy is thinking and feeling. Those wishing to learn the principles of military strategy are not, however, encouraged to feel sympathy for the enemy.

Empathy in Psychoanalysis

Freud mentions the importance of empathy in the practice of psychoanalysis, but briefly and without elaboration (Freud 1913). The importance of empathy and its use in psychiatric practice was eventually recognized and treated as a subject matter in its own right. Racker makes a distinction between *Concordant* and *Complimentary* empathy (Racker 2007). Concordant empathy is employed by the psychoanalyst to identify with the patient; complimentary empathy is used to empathize with the patient's objects. Stressing that the analyst must remain objective even when with the patient, Greenson draws a distinction between what he calls "*identification empathy*" and "*differentiated empathy*" (Greenson 1967). Because empathy is transient in nature (identification empathy), empathy must be employed in a disciplined manner (differentiated empathy). Only by maintaining distance while practicing empathy can the analyst come to understand the patient's thoughts and feelings.

The role of empathy in psychoanalysis has been elaborated by Buie, who recognizes four types of empathy to be used by the analyst (Buie

1981). The first is *Conceptual Empathy*, and it is focused on the analyst's cognitive understanding of the patient, the "model" of the patient's psyche that the analyst has developed over time. It is not based on the emotional dimension of empathy.

The second type Buie calls "*Self-Experiential Empathy*," which is similar to conceptual empathy but contains an emotional component. It occurs when something in the patient's emotional life triggers a similar emotion in the analyst. He illustrates this idea by talking about how the sadness in a patient triggered similar feelings in the therapist: "The therapist realized that his empathic sadness was his own, arising from a similar enough experience in his childhood which… was stirred mildly by his patient's experience." Despite his emotional response, the therapist maintained his conceptual framework he has of the patient. Thus, the therapist "noticed that his empathic response contained conceptual elements too" (Buie 1981:299).

The third type of empathy Buie calls *Imaginative Imitation Empathy*. This occurs when the analyst has no experiences that he could use to feel empathy for the patient. In Buie's example, the analyst had to rely on his imagination so he could empathize with a female patient who experienced sexual trauma as a four-year old girl. The analyst "had to imagine himself anatomically and emotionally as a little girl going through all the details of her excitement, trauma, humiliation, and rage. He also had to imagine himself as a grown woman living with the neurotically elaborated sequela" (Buie 1981:300). This type of empathy requires imagination and creativity as well as discipline.

The fourth and final type of empathy identified by Buie is *Resonant Empathy*. In this example, the patient is releasing repressed feelings of sadness: "Eventually she filled much of several analytic hours with open sobbing. As the analyst listened, he found himself also purely sad; tears often rolled freely down his cheeks. This was not a sadness of his own, and it was not sympathy" (Buie 1981:300). This is a passive form of empathy in which the analyst allows himself to be moved by the patient's emotional state.

Kohut also considers empathy a necessary condition for the practice of psychoanalysis (Kohut 1959). He makes three points regarding the importance of empathy: first, the analyst has to honestly look at his own experience, especially all his losses and defeats. Kohut calls this empathy by the analyst *vicarious introspection*; the analyst feels the patient's pain as best he can and looks inside for an analogous experience or feeling.

Kohut's second point is that the analyst's empathy is composed of two parts, *affect* and *cognition*. Affect is when the analyst sees his patient in pain and looks into his own self to find a similar experience. Cognition happens immediately after affect, and is simply the intellectual recognition that the patient is in pain.

The third point Kohut makes about empathy is simply its importance in inducing the patient to drop his defenses and open up emotionally.

CLINICAL CASES

Kevin

Kevin is a 52 year old man referred for medication management and weekly therapy. He complained of lifelong feelings of sadness and depression. He has a Masters in Social Work, but often talked of how he should have gone to an Ivy League school and gotten a doctorate in psychology. A constant theme of Kevin's was that he felt he had accomplished nothing in life.

He was also having marital problems. He had been married for ten years and had an eight year old son. Kevin said he was no longer attracted to his wife, who had been beautiful when they married but had since gained weight. In addition, Kevin's wife had an affair with his best friend early in their marriage. He was, however, quite close to his son.

Then there is the issue of Kevin's vision, which has been poor his entire life. At age two, he was diagnosed as having only light sensitivity in one eye and severely impaired vision in the other. Kevin expressed feelings of anger, helplessness, and shame over his condition, and had wrestled with these feelings throughout his childhood. Kevin felt inferior to people with "normal" vision and like less of a person because of it. He had difficulty reading menus posted on walls and left coffee shops with the wrong drink because he couldn't read the name written on the cup. He was having trouble finding a job as a social worker, and believed it was because the hospitals where he was applying did not want to make special accommodations for him. Kevin also believed his wife's infidelity was related to his vision problems.

Initially I was able to empathize with Kevin and the problems he faced. Before long, however, Kevin's behavior brought up significant counter-transference. The problems began when Kevin refused to pay his insurance copayments. Every time I brought up the issue, he would accuse me of "caring only about money." In addition, he wanted me to help him get a job as a social worker at an area hospital. He seemed to think that I could just pick up the phone and tell someone to hire him. For me to even try to help him get a job would be unethical. My role as a therapist is to analyze the meaning behind his desire. But that did not stop him from asking. Every time I tried to explore his desire for me to find a job for him, he would get angry and then furious.

Then I informed him that I was no longer accepting private insurance. Kevin immediately became hostile, trying to talk me into continuing his treatment. Eventually he gave up, and began seeing the therapist I referred him to. Kevin still owes me money for unpaid copayments. He also owes money to the therapist to whom I referred him.

Kevin wanted to undergo psychoanalysis, but the prognosis for that option was poor because he has severe (high level) narcissistic personality organization along with poor ego strengths. Patients with this condition are incapable of feeling empathy, and the ability to empathize with others is necessary for someone to undergo analysis. Kevin's lack of empathy manifested in his refusal to make his copays and in his insistence that I help him get a job.

This case demonstrates how important empathy is in the treatment of mental illness.

Mandy

One day I received a phone call from a man named Mandy who requested a consultation visit. He stated that he was having trouble with mental clarity and focus, and thought he might have ADHD. This raised red flags, because it is not uncommon for people to "doctor shop" to obtain stimulants. Because of their addictive properties, I have a policy of judiciously prescribing stimulants to adults. I told him my policy, and he said that he did not want a prescription for stimulants, he just wanted me to find out if he has ADHD.

My initial suspicion, however, proved to be correct: Mandy was addicted to stimulants. He showed up with a long printout from a pharmacy listing all the ADHD prescriptions he had filled over the years. It was a long list; he had been doctor shopping for quite some time. The doctors' names were on the list, and I knew many of them.

Mandy's strategy was to show up with proof of his addiction and ask for a prescription so that he would not go into withdrawal. He was alternative friendly and menacing. He pleaded with me, and when that failed his demeanor changed and he said that if I did not write him a prescription he would go into withdrawal and it would be my fault. In part to prevent him from going into withdrawal and to get him out of my office, I wrote a prescription for seven days of Adderall. Finally, he left my office.

A week later, Mandy called again. He fell over himself apologizing, saying, "I'm so sorry" and "give me another chance." I said no. I told him he needed to go to rehab. Later that day, to my astonishment and annoyance, he showed up at my office—with an enormous German Shepard. I do not consider it a confession to say that I am afraid of dogs, especially big ones. And this dog was *big*.

Showing up at my practice unannounced and without an appointment was completely inappropriate. Showing up with a dog was beyond inappropriate. The entire time Mandy was in my office I was terrified because of that dog. It was clear he was trying to intimidate and bully me into writing him a prescription. I asked him to leave, but he would not. He started to plead his case but I cut him off. I kept telling him to leave and eventually he did, cursing me as he left.

Mandy was not my patient, so there is no way I can formally diagnose him. With that said, based on my brief but memorable interactions with him, he has anti-social personality disorder. In common parlance, Mandy is a sociopath. People like Mandy are incapable of empathy, of putting themselves is another's shoes and trying to see the world the way the other person sees it. Addiction is common among anti-social personalities, as is the non-normative (and intrusive and threatening) behavior exhibited by Mandy.

Richard

Richard was 66 years old when he came to see me. Richard was born in England and had been married for 30 years to a woman four years his senior. Richard reported that his marriage was good and that he loved his wife. They were, however, no longer sexually intimate. He told me that he drank a liter of vodka every day and was, not surprisingly, having issues with his liver. His demeanor and self-presentation gave me the unsettling impression that he did not have long to live.

Richard said he had been depressed for some time, and that his depression was accompanied by feelings of guilt. Before he got married he was in a relationship with an interesting and exciting woman. They travelled the world together for seven years, and he was madly in love with her. They wanted to get married, but Richard had one condition that proved to be a deal-breaker: he absolutely did not want to have children. I never got the full explanation for why he did not want children. He would only say that he had experienced some kind of trauma when he was young.

His girlfriend, however, did want children and when she got pregnant she and Richard were forced to make a decision. She was unwilling to give up her child, so she and Richard parted ways. Richard was devastated and began drinking, a behavior which only worsened over the subsequent 30 years.

Richard settled in the U.S. and got married to a woman who, like him, did not want children. He seemed to love her, but (at least by the time I saw him) in a more platonic than romantic way. She was, of course, 70 years old and he was 66, so passions that may have been present initially had probably faded. At any rate, my conversations with Richard almost always ended with him talking about his seven-year fling with his girlfriend from 30 years ago. And from what he had to say about it, the relationship was indeed exciting. They travelled the world together having outrageous adventures. He was quite obviously nostalgic for his time with her.

It soon became clear that Richard was feeling more than nostalgia. He was feeling a deep sense of loss, even after 30 years. He also felt guilty and regretful, that maybe if he had done something different they could have stayed together. I asked him if he regretted his decision not to have children, and he immediately responded with a resounding,

"No!" So I asked him what he could have done differently, and he acknowledged that unless *she* had decided against having children the outcome would have been the same. But knowing this did not lessen his guilt and sadness.

I found myself moved by his story, thinking of my own loss of a lover because he hadn't wanted to immigrate to the U.S. with me. To my surprise, I was not merely touched by Richard's story but was profoundly moved. I was experiencing a hefty dose of Buie's self-experiential empathy; Richard's story was creating counter-transference that was much more powerful than I would have anticipated.

This perhaps explains what I did next: I explored further and came to the conclusion, which I shared with Richard, that he is having difficulty 30 years later because he is unable to forgive himself. He still feels very guilty about his act. He is terminally ill and I wanted to help him come to terms with that fact and to help him with his guilt.

CHAPTER 12

Shooting For the Divine

To err is human, to forgive divine.
—Alexander Pope

Never does the human soul appear so strong as when it foregoes revenge and dares to forgive an injury.
—Edwin Hubbel Chapin

F orgiveness as a topic has usually been the purview of ethics and religion, not social science. This is surprising given its importance in all aspects of the human experience. "This omission is puzzling, since issues closely linked to forgiveness (e.g., trauma, mourning, guilt, the need for punishment) have been of utmost concern to psychoanalysis" (Ahktar 2002:176). Forgiveness is also important in all types of relationships, especially intimate ones. When psychoanalysis has focused on forgiveness it "has long focused on discussions of guilt" (Person 2007:389).

The *Merriam-Webster Dictionary* online defines forgiveness as follows: 1a) to give up resentment of or claim to requital; 1b) to grant relief from payment; 2) to cease to feel resentment against an offender. These definitions are useful for everyday purposes but are inadequate for the goals of psychoanalysis. Therefore, I offer the following as a psychoanalytical definition of forgiveness:

> *Forgiveness is a conscious and thoughtful act of letting go of resentment and anger towards a person who one believes has done one harm accompanied by a change in attitude towards the offending person. Forgiveness may or may not be accompanied with reparations and/or reconciliation.*

This definition recognizes that forgiveness is a choice and an action, and highlights the change in the victim's attitude towards the offender. It also recognizes that forgiveness does not necessarily entail reparations or reconciliation: forgiveness is not dependent on the perpetrator paying back the victim, nor does it mean that the parties are reconciled. The absence of resentment does not mean that good feelings exist between parties nor that the previous relationship has been restored. The relationship may no longer exist.

Conditions for Forgiveness

One necessary condition for forgiveness is perhaps the most difficult to achieve: agreement on whom was wronged by who. Although this may seem obvious, agreement on this point is often difficult and failure to reach it has prevented many potential acts of forgiveness. If the parties have been in conflict for months or years, "who started it" often becomes a point of contention that stops the process of forgiveness before it can begin. Certain international conflicts are examples of this phenomenon, e.g. the Israeli-Palestinian conflict. Both sides claim to have been the initial occupants of the disputed territory. (For the sake of argument, "the disputed territory" refers to all of Israel and Palestine combined.) In this case, both sides have lived in the territory for so long that the question "who was there first" is impossible to answer meaningfully.

The above is a gross oversimplification of a complex and multifaceted conflict, but it illustrates the difficulty encountered when trying to determine who was wronged. Peace between Israelis and Palestinians is possible without resolving who first occupied the disputed territory. In interpersonal relationships, however, there can be no forgiveness unless the parties agree who is the victim and who is the perpetrator. Agreement is the most important factor here, not its veracity. It may in fact be a fiction, but if so it is a necessary fiction.

Attributes Necessary for the Offender

People asking for forgiveness must possess or adopt certain attributes if they are to be forgiven. Most important is the ability of offenders to feel remorse. Offenders must feel guilty about what they have done, i.e. they must have a conscience. Sociopaths can feign guilt and convince the victim that their remorse is genuine, but if forgiveness is unwittingly given to a sociopath—even if the victim experiences their feigned remorse as genuine—the forgiveness is based on a lie and is not real in any meaningful sense.

In addition to feeling remorse, offenders must be willing to ask for forgiveness as opposed to passively waiting for it to be offered. Genuine forgiveness requires that the request be sincere, which also increases the likelihood that it will be given. If the offender realizes the value of the person he wronged and the importance of that person in his life, the request is sincere and the forgiveness (if given) is real and meaningful.

Third, offenders must be able to understand the damage and hurt they have caused their victims. They must reflect on how and why their behavior led to the victim's pain. This must be a serious rumination, not a cursory thought or fleeting cognition. If the perpetrator is to meaningfully take responsibility for his actions, he must understand how and why he acted as he did. Complete self-understanding is neither necessary nor likely. To misappropriate Winnicott, a "good enough" self-understanding is sufficient. But if the offender truly wants to be forgiven, they must take full responsibility for their actions.

Lastly, perpetrators must own the aspect of their psyche that led them to wrong another. It must not be disavowed or its existence denied. Offenders are unlikely to succeed in eliminating this part of themselves anyway. It is more likely that they will continue to deny its existence and to rationalize similar behavior in the future. Accepting and maintaining an awareness of what led them to wrong the victim makes it less likely that they will repeat the behavior—and more likely that they will be forgiven.

Attributes Necessary for the Victim

The victim's most important attribute is his capacity to forgive the perpetrator. He must be capable of seeing other people as a combination of good and bad qualities, of particular strengths and weaknesses. The victim must not engage in "splitting," in seeing the perpetrator in black and white terms, as all good or all bad.

Next, the victim must decide if the incident was an isolated act or part of a larger pattern. If it was an isolated act, then forgiveness is possible. The situation is different if the incident was not isolated but part of a pattern of wrongs inflicted by the offender. If the act is part of serial behavior by the offender it is likely to happen again, and forgiveness should not be given. The offender may be granted conditional forgiveness (which is not real forgiveness), dependent on the offender's future behavior.

The victim must also decide if he is dealing with a sociopath or a genuinely evil person. If the victim is dealing with a sociopath, the healthiest and safest course of action (if feasible) is to cut all ties with that person. Sociopaths have no remorse, and although they may request forgiveness, receiving it means nothing to them. Ultimately, neither does the victim.

Related to this is the necessity of trying to understand why the offender behaved the way he did. Complete understanding is unlikely; again, a "good enough" understanding of the perpetrator's motives is sufficient for the purpose of determining whether or not to grant forgiveness. The issue of greatest importance is understanding the person well enough to know if his behavior is serial in nature and, more importantly, if the person is capable of feeling remorse.

It is important that the victim not hold a grudge. There can be no real forgiveness if the person who was wronged ostensibly forgives the perpetrator but harbors resentments, which are likely to surface at some point in the future. If the victim is capable of not holding a grudge, he is probably capable of eventually trusting the person again and forgiving himself for having been wronged by the perpetrator.

Intention, Consequence, and Forgiveness

The discussion above assumed that perpetrators commit an offense against their victims that is injurious in nature and which by definition makes one person an offender and the other a victim. The offending behavior can occur in a single instance or serially over time. The offender and victim must demonstrate (different) attributes and capacities if the offender is to be forgiven. A further distinction regarding wrongful acts is, however, necessary to understand whether the victim should or should not forgive the offender.

The distinction is between the perpetrator's wrongful act and its lasting consequences on the victim and provides the basis for the victim's choice whether or not to forgive the offender. When referring to wrongful acts, the important variable is the motivation of the perpetrator. Was the act intentional or was it unintentional? Was the offender fully conscious of what he was doing, or was he motivated by some aspect of their unconscious psyche? As discussed above, the victim must try to answer these questions as best he can, hopefully arriving at a "good enough" explanation. Most acts can be forgiven, unless the offender is without remorse.

However, the wrong inflicted on the victim is more than the act itself. What the victim thinks motivated the offender constitutes only part of the decision to forgive, and not the most important part. The lasting consequences of the wrong done to the victim is ultimately the basis for the decision whether or not to forgive the offender. If the offender's wrongdoing causes irreversible damage to the victim, the offender should not be forgiven. Thus, it is the lasting consequences of the offender's act that determines whether he should be forgiven, not his motivations (unless he is a sociopath or truly evil person).

The following case illustrates the above point. A married couple, both of whom worked full-time, hired a nanny to care for their six-year-old daughter, their only child. The nanny had worked for the couple for over three years and had earned their trust. One afternoon the nanny went to pick up the girl at school. As they were walking hand-in-hand to the nanny's car, the girl suddenly broke away and began running towards the street. Before the nanny could catch her, the girl ran into the street, was hit by a car and died instantly. The nanny could only watch in horror.

Was the child's death the fault of the nanny? Judged in terms of the above criteria, the answer is no. The nanny neither intentionally nor unintentionally wronged the child or her parents, nor was she negligent in the performance of her duties. The girl's death was simply a tragic accident. But this fact does not change nor mitigate the long-term consequences suffered by the parents, who were devastated by the death of their only child. In the best case scenario they will be scarred for life. Even if they fully "recover," they will never be the same.

Although the girl's death was a tragic accident that cannot be blamed on the nanny, in my opinion the parents should not forgive her. The consequences for them are too traumatic, and forgiveness would provide them with neither solace nor benefit of any kind. The parents should not, however, hold a grudge against the nanny, hope (or arrange) for her misfortune, or bear her any ill will. The best course of action is for the parents to unequivocally and permanently cut all ties with their (now former) nanny.

Pathologies of Forgiveness

The first pathology of forgiveness is seen in people who are unable to forgive. People exhibiting this pathology fit into one of two categories. First, are people who have been victimized and hold a grudge against the perpetrator that they will not let go of. In refusing to forgive the perpetrator, they are punishing them. Once the offense has been committed, the victim is now in a position of power vis-à-vis the perpetrator. There is an element of sadism in the victim's refusal to forgive the perpetrator, and the victim derives pleasure from withholding forgiveness—unless the perpetrator feels no remorse for hurting the victim.

In the second category are people with paranoid personality disorders, antisocial personality disorders, or the "syndrome of malignant narcissism," all of which are "severe" personality disorders (Akhtar 2002:190). These people hold grudges and often "harbor resentment toward offenders for months, years, and often an entire lifetime" (Akhtar

2002:189). They "are given to chronic hatred," and if they act on feelings of hatred and revenge they do so without moral restraint or limits.

At the other end of the forgiveness spectrum are people who forgive too easily. People with this pathology fit into one of three subcategories. First are the "obsessional neurotics," who are conflict averse and respond to aggression with inauthentic "forgiveness" so that they can avoid feelings of hurt and anger (Akhtar 2002:190). Second are individuals whose victimization appears to have little emotional impact on them, even in cases of severe trauma. The victimization has had an emotional impact, but the emotions are locked in their unconscious. By forgiving too easily they put themselves back in the position they were in when they were victimized. They are unconsciously re-enacting their victimization as a way of working through it and moving on with their lives. Third are individuals with a more severe form of premature forgiveness that is "defect based." These people "lack a 'healthy capacity for indignation' (Howell 1996), and cannot hate (Galdston 1987)." They are needy and dependent, and as a result "they are all too willing to let go of hurts and injustices" (Akhtar 2002:190).

CLINICAL CASES

Lydia

I did not know Lydia when I received an emotional and desperate email from her. She wrote that she was confused, despairing, in need of psychotherapy, and that she wanted to undergo psychoanalysis. Her email listed her website and business address; I went to her website and saw that she was a renowned philosopher who had published extensively. This piqued my curiosity as I wondered why this intelligent and accomplished person was in such despair and why she chose to request psychotherapy with me. At any rate, we set up an appointment and began treatment.

Like me, Lydia was from India. She was four years old when her parents were killed in an automobile accident. She grew up in an orphanage, but was able to emigrate to the U.S. where she attended college, graduated with an advanced degree, and quickly became a successful philosopher and writer. During this time she began therapy with a psychotherapist whom she saw for three years. This therapist was an MSW who claimed to be a trained psychoanalyst, but who turned out to be poorly trained, incompetent, and in consistent violation of the norms of professional conduct. Lydia's "treatment" left her in worse psychological condition than she had been before seeing this therapist.

Lydia's first psychotherapist created an environment in which she played the role of mother to Lydia's emotionally dependent daughter. Not only was this incredibly unprofessional, it violated standards of treatment for all widely accepted methods of psychotherapy. Regardless of their degree (MSW, Ph.D., M.D.) and what school of thought in which they were trained, psychotherapists are obligated to establish an environment where the patient's thoughts, emotions, motivations—the totality of their psyche—can be analyzed and understood. This is only possible if the therapist sets clear boundaries and maintains them over time. The model is medical, not familial; it should be that of doctor-patient, not parent-child.

It is an understatement to say that Lydia's first therapist failed miserably to establish an appropriate treatment environment. Absent from this environment were the necessary boundaries that separate doctor and patient. No responsible psychotherapist would ever touch a patient; Lydia said her therapist touched her in non-sexual but highly inappropriate ways. The therapist hugged and kissed Lydia, and wiped away her tears like a mother would do for a daughter. No responsible psychotherapist creates an environment like this or engages in this type of behavior.

The job of the therapist is to keep the "treatment frame" intact, i.e. to maintain the proper boundaries between therapist and patient. First, Lydia's therapist failed abysmally to maintain proper professional boundaries as discussed above. Second, the therapist "gratified transference" instead of analyzing it. Transference is the emotion the patient projects onto the therapist, and once identified should be the object of analysis. Gratifying transference is when instead of analyzing the transference the analyst enables and furthers it. For example, Lydia as an orphan desired to have a mother; she transferred these feelings onto her therapist. Instead of analyzing these feelings, the therapist played out the role of the mother Lydia never had, thereby gratifying the transference.

Third, Lydia's therapist engaged in "counter-transference re-enactment." Countertransference refers to the thoughts and feelings the therapist projects onto the patient, and like transference should be the object of analysis. Re-enacting countertransference is when the therapist reinforces and enables these emotions instead of analyzing them. For example, I once told Lydia that I was going on vacation for a week. She reacted with great anxiety, imploring me to at least arrange a session or two over the phone. Had I agreed, I would have been enabling Lydia's dependence on me and not understanding the underlying motivations behind her request, furthering my own feelings of wanting to care for Lydia (the countertransference) by playing the role of her caretaker instead of her analyst.

Lydia made no progress during the three years she was in treatment with this woman. Her therapy ended badly, culminating in one of the most egregious examples of professional misconduct that I have ever heard of. In the final months of Lydia's "treatment," she and her therapist were in a state of conflict, with the therapist blaming Lydia for her lack of progress and for terminating her treatment. The last communication Lydia had with the therapist was an email she received in which the therapist unleashed a torrent of personal attacks on her former patient.

Lydia was told that she was a horrible person who engaged in horrible acts, which is the reason her psychotherapy was unsuccessful. Worse than this—truly a tough act to follow—was the fact that Lydia internalized many of these accusations.

My work with Lydia has largely focused on undoing the damage done by her first therapist. When I began treating Lydia, she was angry and depressed, and felt that what had happened with her first therapist was her fault. Fortunately, she is highly intelligent and sufficiently self-aware to see on an intellectual level that she was not responsible for what happened but that it was the fault of her therapist. But intellect does not always match emotion, and much work remains before Lydia's emotions match her intellectual understanding of her therapist's incompetence and misconduct.

As Lydia has begun to stop blaming herself and recognize the responsibility her therapist bears for their disastrous relationship, anger and a desire for revenge are replacing guilt and despair. Although it may not sound like it, this is a positive development. A desire for revenge can be healthy in people who have been victimized (Akhtar 2002:180), as Lydia was by her pervious therapist. Lydia often wonders if her therapist will ever take responsibility for what she did, and periodically feels intense anger and vengeful feelings towards her therapist. She sometimes talks of filing a malpractice suit against her therapist.

Lydia is progressively coming to the conclusion that she has to forgive her former therapist and herself. This is the only way that she can move on with her life and let go of her anger and desire for revenge. This is a difficult process, but Lydia continues the hard work of forgiving.

Francine

Francine was an Emergency Room nurse in her late 50s who had been married for 25 years and had two sons. When I treated her, she was living with her husband and two grown sons in the same house.

Shortly after they were married, Francine's husband began having affairs with other women, including at least one of his own cousins. At one point, he also committed credit card fraud. Eventually he was arrested and charged for having sex with a 16 year old girl. Francine paid for his legal defense and the substantial fine he was required to pay. She had kept him out of jail. She also had come to loathe him.

Francine did not, however, divorce or separate from him as one might expect. She hated him but chose to live with him anyway in order to exact a unique form of revenge. For the next 15 years Francine withheld from her husband all forms of physical affection, including sex. She also spoke to him only when absolutely necessary. According to Francine, her husband endured these conditions because he was frequently unemployed and financially dependent on her, and because she had kept him out of jail, making him feel obligated to stay.

Francine used her unwillingness to forgive her husband as a means to exact revenge. Their marriage began with Francine's husband continually acting in ways that hurt her. She was the victim and he was the perpetrator. By the time Francine came to me for treatment, the roles had been reversed. She was the perpetrator and he was the victim, and it became apparent that Francine's motivation had a sadistic component.

Elizabeth

One Friday evening I received a call from a woman who sounded extremely agitated and wanted to schedule an appointment for later that night. She said she was "in distress," that she had "messed up," that her marriage was "about to collapse," and that she desperately needed my help. She was not one of my clients and I usually do not work on Friday night, but I said yes. Her tone made it clear she was in distress, and I felt (admittedly without evidence) that if I saw her I would not be putting myself in danger and help her stay safe. So I made an appointment for later that night.

Waiting at my office was a professionally dressed businesswoman in her mid-40s who had been married for 15 years and had a teenage daughter. She had a good job and made good money. She said that she had a "great relationship" with her husband but that her marriage was in jeopardy and this was the reason for her anxiety. She had cheated on her husband and was wracked with guilt and the desire to tell him about the affair. I got her to calm down and tell me the whole story.

A few months earlier, Elizabeth met a man at work who she characterized as handsome, charming, and younger than she. He complimented her often, sometimes on her appearance. This was important to Elizabeth because she was overweight and had significant body-image issues. When her husband was away on a business trip, she went to a hotel with her co-worker for a one night stand, which constituted the entire affair.

Elizabeth reported being surprised by her own behavior. During 15 years of marriage she had never cheated on her husband. We agreed that she needed therapy in order to understand why she had the affair. She told me that her young co-worker made her feel valued and desirable. This partly explained her behavior because of her issues with weight and body-image.

At one point she asked me pointedly if she should tell her husband or just say nothing and let the incident fade from memory. Analyst are not supposed to give advice but to turn the question back on the patient. So I asked her what she thought she should do. She said that she would tell her husband and accept the consequences, whatever they may be.

Unfortunately for Elizabeth, the consequences were not good. She came in the next week and told me that her husband had left her, saying her affair was an unforgivable breach of trust. I was shaken by this outcome even though the decision had been entirely hers. She had been honest about her behavior and had taken responsibility for it. Why couldn't he forgive her? Why did a single indiscretion have to result in the end of a 15 year-long marriage?

I was left asking myself questions about the nature of commitment, trust, and forgiveness. I also could not help but wonder if telling her husband was not the best choice Elizabeth could have made.

FORGIVENESS AND CHOICE

The capacity to forgive and to ask for forgiveness are essential qualities for both parties in a relationship or marriage. People's innate sexuality and aggression will inevitably lead them to betray their partners or spouses. Whether the person who has been betrayed is willing to forgive depends on the nature of the transgression (among other factors). Elizabeth lost her husband because she was so racked with guilt that she told him about her one night stand. She asked for forgiveness, but he was unwilling to forgive her, and a good marriage came to an end. Elizabeth's husband left her because of a single act of infidelity combined with a strikingly honest confession. He was not my patient, so all I can say is that he chose not to forgive Elizabeth.

The serial betrayals committed by Claire's husband were unforgivable, and it is questionable if he ever sincerely asked for forgiveness. But Claire's hateful and sadistic response was pathological, despite—or because of—the pleasure she derived from it. Divorcing her husband and moving on would have been the healthier choice for her. Nevertheless, she chose to psychologically torture her husband rather than leave him.

For people not suffering from a psychopathology which makes forgiveness problematic, forgiveness is a choice. I think that Elizabeth's husband should have forgiven her, but that is my opinion based on my values and appraisal of the situation. His view of the situation was obviously quite different. Lydia should forgive her former psychotherapist and move on, but that is also my opinion. Whatever universal ethical statements one makes about forgiveness, ultimately it is a choice. Some people will turn the other cheek, others will strike back. It is up to the individual to make that choice.

CHAPTER 13

Mourning

A single person is missing for you, and the whole world is empty.
—Joan Didion

We are never so defenseless against suffering as when we love, never so forlornly unhappy as when we have lost our love object or its love.
—Sigmund Freud

U nlike some of the previous topics in this book, much has been written about the process of mourning. I find the topic of particular importance for personal reasons. As an immigrant from India, I have had to mourn certain aspects of Indian culture that were a part of my identity but which, for a variety of reasons, I separated from my self-definition. Some directly contradicted American norms, and holding on to them would have made adapting to American culture unnecessarily difficult. Others proved to be an impediment to succeeding in American society. At any rate, my own immigration experience taught me things about the mourning process that I would otherwise not have learned.

This chapter focuses on the following questions: First, why do people need to mourn a loss and what psychological processes underlie the mourning process? Second, why are some people able to mourn and move on with their lives while others are unable to let go of the lost object? And third, what pathologies are associated with an inability to mourn and let go of the lost object? Different theories of mourning will be examined in an effort to answer these questions.

Auchincloss and Samberg define mourning as follows:

> Mourning or grief is a painful intrapsychic process that occurs in response to the loss of an important object relationship or any other emotionally significant loss such as a job, a possession, an ideal, or one's health or youth (Auchincloss and Samberg 2012:159).

Three aspects of this definition should be emphasized and elaborated. First is the importance of the emotional attachment that one has to the lost object. A person who has been married for a long time but no longer loves his spouse is likely to experience less grief than someone who has only been married a short time but is deeply attached to his partner. Second, when a person is attached to an object, that object is meaningful to that person. The greater the attachment, the greater the meaning the object has for the individual and the greater will be the individual's grief at the loss of the object. The third and final point is the power of the pain people feel when grieving a loss, a pain that frequently is strong enough to induce long-lasting—if not permanent—psychopathology.

Understanding mourning

Much has been written about grief and mourning from psychological and psychoanalytic perspectives. This literature seeks to answer the question of what is really happening when a person mourns a loss. Some theories distinguish between healthy and unhealthy mourning, and the causes and consequences of each. The theories that have had the greatest impact on my own thinking will be presented below, calling attention to their similarities and differences.

The First Psychoanalyst

Freud was the first to offer a theory of mourning (Freud 1917). In Freud's view, healthy mourning depended on the bereaved successfully detaching themselves from the lost object. The pain of loss and its accompanying ideations are gradually replaced by the loosening of emotional bonds that tied them to the departed. Freud saw mourning as a relatively straightforward process beginning with the pain of grief, followed by a gradual letting go ("decathexis") of the lost object, and ending with acceptance of the loss. The person is then able to move on and—possibly—find a new love (Freud 1917:204-5).

Freud saw depression ("melancholia") that occurred conterminously with mourning as symptomatic of pathology. Freud's implies that a healthy mourning process was of relatively short duration (Freud 1917:203-5). He did not specify a time frame, but eventually a consensus formed within the psychoanalytic community that six months to a year—two at most—was the normal, non-pathological time frame for mourning a major loss, like that of a spouse (Kernberg 2010:601).

Kernberg's Revisions

Kernberg embraced this as the healthy time-frame for mourning, but had a change of heart after the death of his wife (Kernberg 2010:601). Like Freud, Kernberg had considered prolonged depression following a major loss as pathological, caused either by the loss itself or exacerbated by pre-existing pathology. After his loss, Kernberg re-evaluated his analyses of past and current patients who had gone through or were going through the process of mourning.

Kernberg went on to develop a theory of what constitutes healthy mourning. He abandoned the idea that healthy mourning must occur within a specific time frame. He also argued that the loss of a loved one results in permanent changes to the mourner's psyche, affecting all aspects of one's life. Most importantly the mourner's loss changes how the lost object is internalized by the person's ego and superego. Healthy mourning includes incorporation of the lost object's value system and life project into the mourner's own value system and life project. This is accompanied by an increased interest in spiritual matters.

Kerberg's new formulation of healthy mourning points to the idea that mourning has no fixed time frame.

> The objective manifestations of mourning, such as a persistent, low-toned sadness… may have all subsided after a year or two as manifest symptoms… And yet, over many years… this becomes a permanent trait of the personality that… can be triggered at any time, and often catches the mourning person by surprise (Kernberg 2010:612).

In other words, people who have mourned in a healthy manner are still prone to bouts of sadness and depression many years after their loss.

Akhtar and Common Delusions

Salman Akhtar explores how unrealistic idealizations of the lost object can result in delusional modes of thinking that inhibit healthy mourning. Akhtar refers to these modes of thinking as "fantasies" and hypothesizes the existence of two types, the "someday" fantasy and the "if only" fantasy. Both are present in the minds of all people in "subtle and subterranean forms," but become pathological when they "encroach upon the executive functions of the ego" (Akhtar 1996:726).

The "someday fantasy" is a form of magical thinking in which the grieving person believes that the lost object will somehow return to them. It is a delusional view of the future characterized by "unrealistic optimism" and "excessive hope." The "someday fantasy" is a form of denial in which the lost object is idealized and obsessed over, alienating the bereaved from the present and preventing him from enjoying the simple pleasures of life. In the first case study presented below, a man whose wife left him years earlier persists—despite overwhelming evidence to the contrary—in believing that she will return to him.

Akhtar's "if only fantasy" is oriented toward the past, but otherwise has much in common with its "someday" counterpart. The lost object is idealized and obsessed over, and the bereaved obsessively blames himself and others for his loss. "If only" they (or someone else) had done something differently, the lost object would still be present. Obsessive blaming is accompanied by self-pity, often tinged by an element of hatefulness.

Akhtar sees these fantasies as both the result of insufficient mourning and an impediment to healthy mourning. Central to the "someday" and "if only" fantasies are their idealization of the lost object. Unless the person who has experienced the loss can let go of his unrealistic view of the lost object, he will not be able to mourn the loss and move on with his life. Rather, with a "…mixture of ache and expectation," people "…with these fantasies [will] arrive at the psychoanalyst's doorstep" (Akhtar 1996:737-8).

Kubler-Ross and the Five Stages of Grief

In her well-known theory of grief and mourning, Elisabeth Kubler-Ross argues that people grieving a loss go through five stages. Her original theory was based on interviews with and observations of 200 terminally ill patients. Nevertheless, much of it can be applied to people mourning other types of loss.

Kubler-Ross's first stage is denial. This stage is compatible with Akhtar's ideas because intense grief coupled with denial often results in delusional thinking, and people lost in "someday" or "if only" fantasies are denying the reality of their loss. Unlike Akhtar, Kubler-Ross argues that denial is a healthy ego defense: "Denial functions as a buffer after unexpected shocking news, allows the patient to collect himself and, with time, mobilize other, less radical defenses" (Kubler-Ross 1969:35). Denial is only healthy, however, if it is temporary.

Anger is the defense mechanism that follows denial. While it may be "less radical" than denial, it is certainly not as sedate. The "anger, rage, envy, and resentment" that follow denial are frequently directed at family, doctors, and other medical personnel (Kubler-Ross 1969:46). Terminally ill patients obsess over the question, "Why me?" and in their anger lash out at those around them. Eventually their anger subsides, giving way to the third stage of "bargaining." Kubler-Ross says the transition from anger to bargaining is analogous to a small child who asks for something, is told "no" then proceeds to have a temper tantrum. Eventually the child calms down, does something helpful for their caregivers, then asks again, this time nicely. Terminally ill people in this stage often bargain with God, and their request is "almost always [for] the extension of life" (Kubler-Ross 1969:72).

When terminally ill patients can no longer deny their impending death, their "anger and rage will soon be replaced with a sense of loss." This is synonymous with depression, Kubler-Ross's fourth stage. Contrary to popular wisdom, she argues that for terminally ill patients, "too much interference from visitors who try to cheer him up hinders his emotional preparation rather than enhances it" (Kubler-Ross 1969:77). "Patients do best who have been encouraged to express their rage, to cry in preparatory grief, and to express their fears and fantasies" (Kubler-Ross 1977:105). Her argument applies to anyone mourning a loss who is encouraged to "look on the bright side" and to "stay positive," and so on.

The final stage is acceptance. The person has "reached a stage during which he is neither depressed nor angry about his 'fate'… and he will contemplate his coming end with a certain degree of quiet expectation" (Kubler-Ross 1969: 99). A person in the acceptance stage is "almost devoid of feelings," and Kubler-Ross is quick to point out that acceptance is not necessarily a happy condition.

Kubler-Ross's stages are defense mechanisms that help people deal with extremely difficult situations. The stages, "will last for different periods of time and will replace each other or exist at times side by side." As her terminally ill patients moved through the stages, hope stood out as a constant (Kubler-Ross 1969:122).

Didion's Grief

In *The Year of Magical Thinking*, Joan Didion gives a moving account of her own grief following the deaths of her husband and daughter, which occurred less than one month apart (Didion 2005). Her account reflects many of the points made in the theories of mourning presented above.

Didion's initial response to her husband's sudden death was denial, even as she calmly told her brother of her husband's death. "I was myself in no way prepared to accept this news as final: there was a level on which I believed that what had happened remained reversible" (Didion 2005:32). Didion also enacted a version of Akhtar's "someday" fantasy. Friends and family implored her to give away her husband's clothes as a way to get over her grief. She resisted, calling these efforts "good natured but misguided." She kept his clothes as part of a fantasy that somehow he would return. Didion also suffered the delusion of the "if only" fantasy, thinking that if only she had done something differently her husband would still be alive.

Didion expresses her disdain for the cultural norm against self-pity. She writes, "In fact the grieving have urgent reasons, even an urgent need, to feel sorry for themselves… We are repeatedly left… with no further focus than ourselves, a source from which self-pity naturally flows" (Kubler-Ross 1969:195). In other words, self-pity is a normal part of the grieving process and the mourner should be allowed to express it without reproach. This echoes Kubler-Ross's criticism of those who exhort the grieving not to be angry, depressed, or "negative."

CLINICAL CASES

Priya

Priya was a woman of Indian descent in her late twenties, single with a 3 month-old son. The child's father was Priya's Indian-born boyfriend Samir, who owned a small business but was not well-educated. They were in love and wanted to get married, but Priya's parents did not approve of Samir because he was poorly educated and was in the U.S. illegally. They demanded that she cut all ties with him. When Priya refused, her family cut most ties with her, refusing to support her in any way or to visit. Occasionally, they would answer her phone calls.

I had been treating Priya for a few months when Samir received a deportation order. He immediately hired a lawyer who successfully got an immigration court to temporarily stop the deportation process. Unfortunately, the Immigration and Customs Enforcement (ICE) agency ignored—or was not informed of—the court's ruling. One morning at 5am, agents from ICE arrested Samir and soon after he was on a plane to India. It was a one-way trip. Samir was told that he would never be allowed to return to the United States, a status that was marked on his passport.

Priya arrived for her next appointment in a state of shock. She was terrified and on the verge of despair. I wrote some prescriptions to help her deal with the situation. After learning what had transpired, I realized that Priya had to choose between two undesirable and harsh options. She could either move to India or accept the fact that Samir was never coming back. Priya grew up in the U.S. and was culturally American. For all intents and purposes, for Priya, India was a foreign country. Permanently expatriating herself to India to be with Samir was as undesirable as never seeing him again.

Ultimately, Priya decided to stay in the U.S. but suffers from profound anxiety and depression. She has not been able to properly mourn the loss of Samir and move on with her life. I see a number of factors contributing to her inability to let go of Samir. First, there is no hope of Samir returning to the U.S., a fact that permeates Priya's psyche, leaving her in a constant struggle against feelings of hopelessness about life in general. Second, Priya has yet to recover from the shock of Samir's deportation, which was completely unexpected given the immigration court's ruling. Priya is plagued by guilt because she did not have an opportunity to even say goodbye; rationally she knows she is not to blame for this but feels guilty nonetheless.

Even before Samir's deportation, Priya felt guilty for having gone against the wishes of her parents. Her parents had warned Priya that marrying Samir would cause her hardship, and she now considered Samir's deportation to be a prophecy come true. This is of course nonsense, but thus far Priya has been unable to recognize it as delusional thinking. She now has a pervasive sense of foreboding about all aspects of her life, including how she will support her son. Priya's belief that her parents' prophesy came true combined with her apprehension about the future constitute the third factor preventing her from mourning the loss of Samir.

Samir is still alive and (hopefully) well in India, as Priya is painfully aware. Priya would probably have an easier time mourning the loss of Samir if he had died. The finality of death makes it more difficult for fantasies to get past the reality-testing aspect of the ego, including fantasies of reuniting with the lost object.

Preet

Preet was born in India, is a naturalized American citizen in his late 50s with two grown sons. When he first came for treatment he was severely depressed. He had been married to his first wife Zoya for 25 years when she died of breast cancer. Zoya had battled the disease for seven years before she died four years ealier. Preet was devastated by her death, and began to drink heavily. One night he attempted suicide. After getting very drunk, he began smashing things in his home with the intention of cutting himself and bleeding to death. Neighbors heard the noise and called the police. Preet was taken to the psychiatric ward of a nearby hospital and was released after a week with the strong recommendation that he seek therapy. He did not follow this recommendation. The hospital that he was taken to was the same one where his Zoya was treated; the significance of this fact will be seen below.

These events occurred approximately four years ago. After being released from the hospital, Preet resumed working. Apart from his absence while in the hospital, his job performance was unaffected. One year after the death of his first wife, he married a co-worker, a subordinate almost 20 years younger than he who, like his first wife, was named Zoya. Preet says that he told Zoya he would be unable to truly love her and that she could never replace his first wife. Zoya accepted this, and the two were married three years ago. Preet was no longer suicidal or depressed, but by no means had he recovered from the loss of his first wife.

Preet's second wife is in the U.S. illegally. In the past, marrying a citizen (like Preet) would automatically make Zoya a U.S. citizen. But Preet consulted an immigration attorney to clarify Zoya's status and was told that it was "complicated" because she had been in the country illegally when they married. Any action taken to clarify her status could draw attention to this fact and possibly result in her deportation. Preet was advised that the best course of action was, at least for now, to do nothing.

Hearing this sent Preet into a downward spiral of depression. He did not go to work for six weeks. When I asked him why his reaction to the news was so strong, he would only say, "I cannot lose Zoya."

Since the death of his first wife, Preet has engaged in behaviors that indicate he has not fully mourned the loss of his first wife. Remarrying a woman with the same name as his first wife was only one such behavior. Other similar behaviors include the following:

- Preet's first wife died at 4am; since then, he has been unable to sleep past 4am.
- Preet has not rid himself of any of his first wife's possessions, including her clothes.
- Since her death he has travelled to India, each time bringing his first wife's saris with him. He holds onto them, then returns to the States with her saris.
- Located close to the hospital where Zoya received her cancer treatment—and where he was taken after his attempted suicide—is a well-known Indian grocery store. Preet always shops there despite the fact it is out of his way.
- Zoya had always expressed the desire to travel to Paris, but died before she could. Years ago, Preet travelled to Paris with her ashes and scattered them in the Seine. This could be seen as

healthy, if not for the other behaviors indicative of incomplete mourning.

In addition, Preet is plagued by losses that he has not fully mourned and which are infused with feelings of guilt. Six months before his first wife died, Preet travelled to India to visit his mother. While he was there, she fell and broke her back. Preet stayed with her as long as he could before returning to the U.S. Shortly after his return, his mother died. Preet is still plagued by guilt because he was not at his mother's side when she passed. Preet's father died a few months before the death of his mother, and Preet feels guilty about this as well. He also believes that he could have done more for his first wife, though he is unable to specify exactly what he could have done.

On top of all this, Preet feels guilty about getting remarried, regarding it as a betrayal of his first wife. This is another strong indication that he has not fully mourned her death. Preet sees that his second wife has had a psychologically stabilizing influence on him, but combined with his guilt over remarrying, he is left feeling ambivalent about his second marriage.

Preet's depression is the result of his guilt, ambivalence, and inability to fully mourn the loss of his mother and father. His depression, in turn, prevents his properly mourning the death of his first wife.

Jason

Jason is an accomplished professional in his 60s who has been married and divorced twice. His first marriage lasted for 25 years, his second for 12. His second wife left him four years ago, a loss that he has been unable to successfully mourn. Akhtar's "if only" fantasy provides the most useful framework for understanding Jason's inability to let go of his second wife.

Jason's second wife "Jane" left him four years ago, but wanted to remain friends. Jason agreed to this arrangement even though he wanted more—he wanted Jane to still be his wife. Since this arrangement was established, Jason has been on a psychological treadmill, trudging through various versions of the "if only" fantasy, believing that if certain conditions are met, Jane would return.

The first of these conditions focused on their dog, which Jane took with her when she left. The dog was old, and shortly after Jane's departure became quite ill. Jane spent much time, energy, and money caring for it. Meanwhile, Jason was expending a great deal of time and energy believing that once the dog died, Jane would return. Jason believed this despite the fact that Jane made it explicitly clear she had no desire to return. Nevertheless, Jason's fantasies of reuniting with his ex-wife persisted. When the dog died and Jane failed to return, Jason's reunification fantasies continued, only with a new "if only" condition. For some time, Jane had been seeing a psychotherapist. Jason believed that when she stopped seeing this psychotherapist, Jane would return. Jane did stop seeing the therapist and of course did not return. Jason quickly created another "if only" condition.

Jason is an intelligent man who is solidly in touch with reality—except when the reality concerns Jane. The goal of treatment was getting Jason to recognize that his thinking was not in touch with the reality that Jane was gone, and that he was continually repeating "if only" and "someday" fantasies. It took a great deal of time and effort, but gradually he came to see that his thinking was divorced from reality and that he was repeating the "if only" fantasies. This allowed Jason to finally mourn the loss of Jane and move on with his life.

MOURNING AND MOVING ON

The importance of healthy mourning can be seen in each of the cases above. Only Jason—after four years—was able to let go of his delusion that Jane would return and move on with his life. Priya needs to mourn the loss of Samir, something I am not sure she will be able to do. If she does, it will probably take a long time. Meanwhile, Preet remains unable to grieve the loss of his first wife and is plagued by guilt. If Priya and Preet remain unable to fully mourn the loss of their love objects, they will be unable to move on with their lives—which includes the formation of new relationships.

Relationships are not the only psychological process that incomplete mourning interferes with. In the process of redefining herself—necessitated by her immigration to the U.S.—Sarah had to redefine herself. By any measure her redefinition was radical; among other major changes, she dropped her Muslim identity. Sarah could not have done this without mourning the loss of her religion, as well as the other aspects of herself that she chose to change (and those that changed without a conscious decision on her part). As stated earlier, some of these changes were necessary to adapt to a culture very different from the one she grew up in. Had she not been able to mourn the various losses of her self-definition, she would not have been able to adapt to life in America.

The inability to fully mourn a loss can be a matter of life and death. Preet nearly eviscerated himself out of grief over the loss of his first wife. If Priya is unable to mourn the loss of Samir, at the very least she will be unable to form a new love relationship; at worst, her life could degenerate in a way similar to Preet's. If Jason had not broken out of his delusional "someday" and "if only" fantasies, he would still be wasting his life thinking that Jane would return if only she did this or that thing.

Healthy and stable marriages depend on the absence of continuing and pervasive grief. Losses and the grief that comes with them are simply part of life and cannot be avoided. But unabated grief and the incomplete mourning that goes with it will inevitably interfere with the formation of new relationships, romantic and otherwise.

CONCLUSION

The ties that bind husband and wife are tightest in arranged marriages. There is little need to maintain "commitment," as this is guaranteed by the patriarchy of the culture acting through the husband, the family, and the community, with violence as the ultimate mechanism of enforcement. Like Sarah, I have felt nostalgic for arranged marriages, but only because I would be free of having to find a suitable mate. My nostalgia quickly fades when I remember what these marriages were actually like.

The title of this book has a double meaning: the "Marital Knot" refers—in a positive way—to the ties that bind husband and wife together. The other meaning is a knot that can tie marriage partners too close and suffocate one or both. Or, it can refer to a noose one would use to hang oneself. The clinical cases presented above are primarily examples of the latter.

There is a vision of marriage that is more positive, part of which was presented in chapter three. It is of a "Marital Knot" that is neither too loose nor too tight, and certainly does not drive one or both partners to tie a noose. The realization of this vision is quite improbable in an arranged marriage, as it would largely depend on luck. It is possible in love marriages, though its attainment is difficult and requires hard work and wise choices. This picture of the ideal marriage is beautifully expressed in the following poem by Kahlil Gibran:

Let there be spaces in your togetherness,
And let the winds of the heavens dance between you.

Love one another but make not a bond of love:
Let it rather be a moving sea between the shores of your souls.

Fill each other's cup but drink not from one cup.
Give one another of your bread but eat not from the same loaf.

Sing and dance together and be joyous, but let each one of you be
    alone,
Even as the strings of a lute are alone though they quiver with the
    same music.

Give your hearts, but not into each other's keeping.
For only the hand of Life can contain your hearts.

For the pillars of the temple stand apart,
And the oak tree and the cypress grow not in each other's shadow.

The upshot is that marriage partners should be bound together, but not too tightly. Gibran's poem echoes Akhtar's "optimal space," and suggests Kernberg's notions of basic trust, forgiveness, and gratitude. The ideal Marital Knot is tied neither too tightly nor too loosely, binding husband and wife together but giving them freedom to be themselves and to define themselves. A union such as this is not arrived at easily; in addition to hard work and wise choices, it depends on a degree of good fortune and good luck.

About the Author

 Shabnamzehra Bhojani, M.D. is an Indian-born psychiatrist who lives and works in New York City. Before immigrating to the United States, Dr. Bhojani received a full scholarship to attend the Government Medical College in Miraj, India, where she earned her M.D. She completed her residency in psychiatry at Jamaica Hospital Medical Center, followed by a Fellowship in Child and Adolescent Psychiatry at Mount Sinai School of Medicine, both located in New York City. Dr. Bhojani is Board Certified in Psychiatry and Neurology as well as Child and Adolescent Psychiatry. She is currently a Candidate in Psychoanalytic Training at Columbia University Medical Center.

Dr. Bhojani is founder and CEO of Healthy Minds Physicians in Forest Hills, NY, where she practices psychoanalysis, intensive psychoanalytic psychotherapy, and medication management. She also conducts forensic psychiatric evaluations for the criminal justice system, including civil, criminal, child custody, and immigration cases. In addition, she is Medical Director of the Advocate Center for Queens, New York, which treats opiate and other drug addictions.

Dr. Bhojani speaks English, Hindi, Urdu, Gujarati, and Marathi. She lives in Queens, New York.

Acknowledgements

I would like to thank my editor, Douglas Wiese, for encouraging me while also tactfully providing critical commentary on my work. Receiving clear and honest feedback was of particular importance because English is my second language. It helped make the writing of this book a wonderful learning experience.

References

Akhtar, Salman. 1996. "Someday…" and "If Only…" Fantasies: Pathological Optimism and Inordinate Nostalgia as Related Forms of Idealization. *Journal of the American Psychoanalytic Association* 44:723-753.

Akhtar, Salman. 1999. *Inner Torment: Living Between Conflict and Fragmentation*. New York: Roman and Littlefield, Inc.

Akhtar, Salman. 2002. Forgiveness: Origins, Dynamics, Psychopathology, and Technical Relevance. *Psychoanalytic Quarterly* 71:175-212.

Akhtar, Salman. 2014. *Sources of Suffering: Fear, Greed, Guilt, Deception, Betrayal, and Revenge*. London: Karnac Books.

Allison and Risman, 2014. It Goes Hand in Hand with the Parties. *Sociological Perspectives* 57(1): 102-123.

Arendt, Hannah. 1964. *Eichmann in Jerusalem: A Report on the Banality of Evil*. Harmonsworth, NY: Penguin Books.

Auchincloss, Elizabeth and Eslee Samberg. 2012. *Psychoanalytic Terms and Concepts*. New Haven: Yale University Press.

Beattie, Hillary J. 2005. Revenge. *Journal of the American Psychoanalytic Association* 53(2): 513-524.

Bollas, Christopher. 1984. Loving Hate. *Annual of Psychoanalysis* 12:221-237.

Bowlby, John. 1969. *Attachment and Loss*. New York: Basic Books.

Buie, Dan. 1981. Empathy: Its Nature and Limitations. *Journal of the American Psychoanalytic Association* 29:281-307.

Chodorow, Nancy. 1999. *The Reproduction of Mothering: Psychoanalysis and the Sociology of Gender*. Berkeley: University of California Press.

Clausewitz, Carl von. 1916. *On War*. Berlin: M. Warnec.

Crabb, George. 1917. *Crabb's English Synonyms*. London: Harper and Brothers.

Didion, Joan. 2005. *The Year of Magical Thinking*. New York: Knopf.

Downey, T. Wayne. 2004. Notes on Hate and Hating. *Psychoanalytic Study of the Child* 59:3-20.

DSM-5. 2013. *Desk reference to the diagnostic criteria from DSM-5, American Psychiatric Association*. American Psychiatric Publishing.

Erikson, Erik. 1950. *Childhood and Society*. New York: W. W. Norton and Company, Inc.

Freud, Sigmund. 1917. *Mourning and Melancholia*. New York: Penguin Books.

Freud, Sigmund. 1920. *Beyond the Pleasure Principle*. New York: Liveright.

Freud, Sigmund. 1930. *Civilization and its Discontents*. New York: W.W. Norton.

Friedman, Richard C. 2010. Review of: The Anatomy of Evil by Michael H. Stone. *Journal of American Academy of Psychoanalysis* 38:361-362.

Gabbard, Glen O. and Jerome A. Winer. 1994. Hate in the Analytic Setting. *Journal of the American Psychoanalytic Association* 42:219-231

Galdston, Richard. 1987. The Longest Pleasure: A Psychoanalytic Study of Hatred. *International Journal of Psycho-Analysis* 68:371-378.

Gay, Peter. 1989. *Freud: A Life for our Time*. New York: Anchor Books.

Gershman, H. 1947. Neurotic Pride and Self-Hatred According to Freud and Horney. *American Journal of Psychoanalysis* 7:53-55.

Greenson, 1967. *The Technique and Practice of Psychoanalysis*. New York: International Universities Press.

Hartman, Heinz, Ernst Kris, and Rudolph M. Lowenstein. 1949. Notes on the Theory of Aggression. *Psychoanalytic Study of the Child* 3:9-36.

Hering, Christoph. 1997. Beyond Understanding? Some Thoughts on the Meaning and Function of the Notion of "Evil." *British Journal of Psychotherapy* 14:209-220.

Horne, Michael. 2008. Evil Acts not Evil People: Their Characteristics and Contexts. *Journal of Analytical Psychology* 53:669-690.

Kernberg, Otto. 2010. Some Observations on the Process of Mourning. *International Journal of Psycho-Analysis* 91(3):601-619.

Kernberg, Otto. 2012. *The Inseparable Nature of Love and Aggression. Clinical and Theoretical Perspectives*. London: American Psychiatric Publishing.

Klein, Melanie. 1975. *Envy and Gratitude, and Other Works, 1946-1963*. New York: Free Press.

Kohut, Heinz. 1959. Introspection, Empathy, and Psychoanalysis: An Examination of the Relationship Between Mode of Observation and Theory. *Journal of the American Psychoanalytic Association* 7:459-483.

Kubler-Ross, Elisabeth. 1969. *On Death and Dying*. New York: Macmillan.

Mahler, Margaret, with Fred Pine and Anni Bergman. 1985. *The Psychological Birth of the Human Infant; Symbiosis and Individuation*. London: Karnac Books.

Martin, Andres, and Fred R. Volkmar. 2007. *Lewis's Child and Adolescent Psychiatry: A Comprehensive Textbook*. Philadelphia: Wolters Kluwer Health, Lippincott Williams & Wilkins.

Person, Ethel Spector. 2007. Forgiveness and its Limits: A Psychological and Psychoanalytic Perspective. *Psychoanalytic Review* 94:389-408.

Piaget, Jean. 1966. *The Psychology of Intelligence*. Totowa, N.J.: Littlefield, Adams & Co.

Racker, Heinrich. 2007. The Meanings and Uses of Countertransference. *Psychoanalytic Quarterly* 76(3): 725-777.

Rosen Irwin C. 2007. Revenge—the Hate That Dare Not Speak its Name: A Psychoanalytic Perspective. *Journal of the American Psychoanalytic Association* 55:595-619.

Stone, Michael H. 2009. *The Anatomy of Evil*. Amherst, N.Y.: Prometheus Books.

Tzu, Sun. *Sun-tzu on the Art of War: The Oldest Military Treatise in the World*. Boulder, CO: Wiretap.

Tannen, Deborah. 1990. *You Just Don't Understand*. New York: Ballantine.

Winnicott, D.W. 1957. *The Child and the Outside World*. London: Tavistock.

Winnicott, D.W. 1971. *Therapeutic Consultations in Child Psychiatry*. New York: Basic Books.

Oxford English Dictionary. Online: www.oed.com.

Merriam-Webster Dictionary. Online: www.merriam-webster.com.

Morgan James
Speakers Group

www.TheMorganJamesSpeakersGroup.com

We connect Morgan James published
authors with live and online events
and audiences who will benefit
from their expertise.

Morgan James makes all of our titles available
through the Library for All Charity Organization.

www.LibraryForAll.org

Printed in the USA
CPSIA information can be obtained
at www.ICGtesting.com
JSHW082348140824
68134JS00020B/1953